COUNT YOUR

BLESSINGS

~

COUNT YOUR BLESSINGS

~

63 Things *to be* Grateful *for in* Everyday Life . . .
and How *to* Appreciate Them

ROBERT W. BLY

THOMAS NELSON PUBLISHERS®
Nashville

A Division of Thomas Nelson, Inc.
www.ThomasNelson.com

Published in Nashville, Tennessee, by Thomas Nelson, Inc.

Scripture quotations are from THE NEW KING JAMES VERSION. Copyright © 1979, 1980, 1982, Thomas Nelson, Inc., Publishers.

ILibrary of Congress Cataloging-in-Publication Data

Bly, Robert W.
    Count your blessings : 63 things to be grateful for in everyday life--
and how to appreciate them / Robert W. Bly.
        p. cm.
    ISBN 0-7852-6621-6 (pbk.)
    1. Conduct of life. 2. Gratitude. I. Title.
BJ1581.2 .B56 2002
179'.9--dc21

                                        2002003169

Printed in the United States of America
02 03 04 05 06 PHX 5 4 3 2 1

In memory of the victims

of the anti-U.S. terrorist attacks

on September 11, 2001

Contents

~

If all our misfortunes were laid in one common heap, whence everyone must take an equal portion, most people would be content to take their own and depart.

—SOLON (C. 630–560 B.C.), STATESMAN

INTRODUCTION

~

DIFFICULTIES EXIST TO BE SURMOUNTED. THE GREAT heart will no more complain of the obstructions that make success hard, than of the iron walls of the gun which hinder the shot from scattering. It was walled round with iron tube with that purpose, to give it irresistible force in one direction. A strenuous soul hates cheap success.

—RALPH WALDO EMERSON, POET

Sorrow and joy are yoked together not for contrast but because they are different expressions of the same physiological condition. It is a fallacy to assume that sorrow implies evil and that joy represents happiness, for even in laughter the heart is sad and the end of joy is heaviness.

Legend tells of the woman who came to the river Styx to be ferried across to the land of departed spirits. Charos, the ferryman, offers her a certain potion which can cause her to forget the life she is leaving and all of its sorrows. In the end, the woman leaves the draught untasted, choosing to remember life's pains and sorrows and failures rather than to forget its joys, its triumphs, and its loves. Sorrow and joy belong together. They are precious experiences which deepen understanding and give meaning to life.

—PAUL S. MCELROY, *QUIET THOUGHTS*

"This earthly life is a battle," said Ma. "If it isn't one thing to contend with, it's another. It always has been so, and it always will be. The sooner you make up your mind to that, the better off you are, and the more thankful for your pleasures."

—LAURA INGALLS WILDER, *LITTLE TOWN ON THE PRAIRIE*

Your entire life can change in one instant, but how you handle this one instant is up to you. Like my grandmother used to say, "Is the glass half full, or half empty?" I'll take the half-full glass over the half-empty glass every time.

—LAURIE CORNELL, *THE PARENT PAPER*

Everybody has problems, but everybody also has blessings in life. Depression and despair come from perceiving that the problems outweigh the benefits, which often occurs when one or more of the problems is severe.

But an objective look at life shows that, in the overwhelming majority of cases, the total good of the blessings far outweighs the negatives of the problems. If one can see this clearly—and practice "the attitude of gratitude"—one can be happy, motivated, enthusiastic, and strong.

As Solon noted more than five centuries before the birth of Christ: If all of us on the planet put our troubles in a big pile, and then were given the choice of taking out an equal portion of the world's problems or just taking back what we put in, most of us would choose the latter.

The problem is, many people cannot see this truth at certain times in their lives. And there has been no book to help them do so. Until now.

Count Your Blessings works on two levels. First, it presents a compilation of some of the many blessings most of us have in our everyday lives but often overlook, and discusses the value and significance of these blessings. Some are admittedly fun, lighthearted, perhaps even trivial. Others are weighty and serious. All are my personal choices; your list might be different. Whatever your blessings may be, I hope that reading this book will make you appreciate what you have more and that you will feel more blessed.

In this book, I have given you only a starting point for counting your blessings. But if you and your family spend a few evenings discussing your blessings at dinner, I guarantee you will compile a list far longer than mine.

Second, *Count Your Blessings* has a scoring system that proves to readers that their blessings outweigh their burdens. How does it work?

Simple. First, count up all the blessings mentioned in this book.

Next, write additional blessings in your life in the space provided. If you come up with less than two dozen, you're probably missing some. Think about it some more until you add at least half a dozen new items to your list. (Are you able to sit in a chair, read this paragraph, and ponder your answer? You've just mentioned three blessings.)

Now add the total of all the blessings listed, and use the self-scoring system that follows. You will soon see that—even if life seems bleak—there are many rays of sunshine, many things worth living for.

When I was growing up, whenever something bad happened to one of us in my family, my mother's strategy was to console us with the knowledge that it could have been much worse. If someone broke an arm, she would say, "At least you didn't break your leg." If someone broke a leg, she'd tell us to thank God it wasn't both legs.

Then I grew up and, at age twenty-six, got married. A few months after our wedding, my wife was diagnosed with thyroid cancer. "At least it wasn't lung or brain cancer," my mother said to console me, and with a start I realized she was right.

Amy was treated successfully and, after eighteen years of marriage and giving birth to our two sons, remains cancer-free today. If you're a spouse or a parent, you know that neither role is easy. But no matter what the problems are on any given day, I am eternally grateful that they are not worse.

Our older son, for example, was diagnosed with Attention Deficit Disorder (ADD), and dealing with ADD on a daily basis can be exhausting. Sometimes Alex challenges us, but every day I thank God that he is healthy, smart, and relatively happy.

"Count your blessings" is such a common expression that it has become a catchphrase. Yet it contains powerful truth and meaning: Be grateful for what you have—and for what you don't have. Everyone has problems, but they could be a thousand times worse—as the tragic attacks of September 11, 2001 on the World Trade Center and, the Pentagon have so dramatically illustrated. *Count Your Blessings* gives readers a simple tool for transforming this simple phrase into greater happiness, contentment, joy, and action.

Scoring System

~

WITH A PENCIL, PUT A LIGHT CHECK MARK NEXT TO every item on the Contents pages for which you are personally grateful.

Next, make your own list of blessings not included in my list. Write down everything positive in your life you can think of.

Now count the total and read your score below:

# OF BLESSINGS:	WHAT IT MEANS:
50 or more	*You are incredibly blessed! You have a life most others would envy.*
30 – 49	*Your life is abundant with blessings. A few things could be better, but that's true with everybody. By and large, you're living the good life.*
10 – 29	*You're luckier than you realize. Yes, life can be difficult. But if everyone in the world laid his/her misfortunes in a heap, would you want to take an equal share? Or would you be content to take back what you put in and go home?*
5 – 9	*Perhaps you have had some serious challenges and struggles—really major stuff. But you're a survivor, and you've survived. Press on. There may be more sorrows to come, but there will also be many joys.*
0 – 4	*It is highly unlikely you counted accurately if your score is below 5. A negative attitude may be clouding your perception of reality. Consider seeing a therapist or doctor; you may be suffering from depression.*

COUNT YOUR

BLESSINGS

~

AIR-CONDITIONING

~

As a cold-weather enthusiast, I believe the world becomes nearly uninhabitable for three months out of every year—namely, summer. And every summer, I close the windows, turn down the thermostat, and thank God for air-conditioning, without which my life would be absolutely miserable during the summer months.

Although the first commercial air conditioner, built by Willis H. Carrier, was an industrial unit installed in a Brooklyn printing plant in 1902, room air conditioners didn't start making it into homes until the 1960s. So I am old enough to remember living in a house without air-conditioning. Can you imagine never being able to get cool and comfortable? That was the way things were in summer.

A friend relates: "We lived in an apartment in the Bronx, and my father worked evenings. I remember him trying to sleep during the day in the summer. The bed would be soaked with sweat, and he would wrap himself with wet towels trying to get cool." Sheer torment.

An air conditioner is like a refrigerator, except it cools the air outside the box instead of inside. The secret is Freon, a refrigerant that makes an endless transition from gas to liquid and back to gas again as it is cycled through the unit.

Like all liquids, Freon absorbs heat as it becomes a gas.

Heat is absorbed from the air, cooling it. As the air cools, it gives off moisture. The moisture condenses, which is why you always see water dripping from air conditioners sticking out of walls and windows.

We often take blessings like air-conditioning for granted—until we don't have them. As I write this, we have just emerged from the most intense heat wave of this summer, which turned most of New Jersey into a steam bath. And we just moved into a new house, in which the central air-conditioning picked this week to fail.

All of us were moaning and groaning. The kids and I complained about the heat; my wife, about the expense of replacing the unit.

Without air-conditioning, the quality of my life was severely compromised. I couldn't sleep, so I was tired the next day and unproductive at work. I couldn't even get close to comfortable in my own home, so I couldn't enjoy simple leisure activities we take for granted, such as reading or watching TV.

But thank God we have the money to buy a new air conditioner. Thank God there is such a thing as an air conditioner to buy.

The installer is almost finished hooking up the unit. Excuse me for a minute while I turn the thermostat down to sixty-eight and indulge my passion for keeping cool.

AMERICA

~

THE UNITED STATES IS LIKE A GIGANTIC BOILER.
Once the fire is lit under it, there is no limit to the power
it can generate.

—WINSTON CHURCHILL

"God bless America," the old song says. And repopularized
in the wake of the tragic terrorist attacks on the World Trade
Center and the Pentagon of September 11, 2001, a more
contemporary song exclaims: "I'm proud to be an
American!" If there is one good thing to come out of 9-11, it
is a renewed national spirit of patriotism and a nationwide
appreciation of the privilege we enjoy living in the greatest
country in the world.

As one anonymous author observes:

What does it mean to be an American? If you ask any of
the more than 280 million citizens of the United States,
chances are you will get more than 280 million unique
answers. But they all will have one common thread running through them—that to be an American is to be free.

Which leads to the question, What is freedom? Most
Americans will say that freedom is the opportunity to
make choices based upon their values, goals, and desires.

Some might say it's the chance to be whoever they want to be. Still others might suggest it is the ability to speak their mind without worry of retribution. Freedom means many things to many people, yet we often neglect to think about what it means to us until there is a threat of it being taken away.

Terrorist actions, war, martial law—these things run rampant in many troubled nations, yet America has had very little experience with challenges to the day-to-day freedoms we exercise without a second thought.

Think about how blessed we are as a nation, as a people, to be free. Free to think, act, speak, and dream with no limitations to what we can accomplish. But in order to keep the freedoms we hold so dear, we must never take them for granted. Honoring and fighting for freedom both here and the world over—that is what it means to be an American.

Books

~

A BOOK THAT INSTRUCTS IN SOME PROFITABLE FIELD is a priceless treasure. It stands patient and mute until you command it to teach. When it teaches, it teaches only as fast as you are capable of learning, and will repeat the difficult parts as often as is necessary to firmly entrench them in your brain. It will never rebuke you for tardiness to class, nor complain under a thousand interruptions. It never forgets even a minor principle of its conceptual message, yet it will not scold you if you forget even major ones. Such a book ranks with a faithful hound as one of man's best friends. If the bookseller offers it and you pass up the chance of ownership, who suffers the most: You? Or the bookseller, who will only sell it to the next one who browses?

—JERRY BUCHANAN

I confess: I'm a bookworm. A bibliophile. A bookaholic. I love books. Always have, always will. Which is why I'm grateful they're still around—and that the Internet has not yet wiped them off the face of the earth.

When I was a college freshman onescore and six years ago, the ambition of many young people my age was to write the Great American Novel, and we spent our formative years seeking agents and publishers.

Today, despite the recent rash of dot.com failures—over two hundred in the year 2000 alone—the current generation's ambition is to start an Internet company, have an IPO, and become billionaires—and they spend their formative years desperately seeking venture capital.

The rise of high-tech to cultural dominance has left me, at forty-four, feeling old and obsolete. My passions—writing, literature, books, the printed word—seem quaintly out-of-date in a world where speed is measured in terabytes per second instead of miles per hour. As a print person, I feel terribly out of the loop; the screen-and-graphics people have taken over the henhouse and now rule the roost.

Increasingly I worry that computers in general—and the Internet in particular—will make print obsolete. Am I just obsessing, or is there real reason for us paper-and-ink addicts to quiver behind our bookmarks? Actually, the news is better than the media would have us think.

Advocates of CD-ROMs, software, the Internet, and electronic publishing are loudly proclaiming, "Print is dead." But futurists have been saying this for a long time—yet so far, it has not come to pass.

When Thomas Edison invented the phonograph (from the Greek words for *sound writing*) in 1876, he did so to bring music into the average American home. In his early model, the "records" were made of cylinders coated with tinfoil, onto which the vibrations from sound waves were impressed with a needle.

Once he got a working device, Edison saw his invention could be used to carry the spoken word as well as music. He publicly proclaimed that the book-on-record—precursor of today's audiobook industry—was a far superior learning tool to the printed page, and that by the end of the millennium, all college students would be learning by listening to recorded texts, and paper textbooks would be obsolete. In 1996, however, textbook sales in the United States grossed over $4 billion.

In 1964, when Sony introduced the CV-2000, the first home VCR, technologists proclaimed that the new videocassettes heralded the death of the printed word. Futurist and science-fiction author Isaac Asimov responded with an essay describing what he called "the ultimate cassette."

Such a cassette, said Asimov, would be lightweight and portable. It would not require a player or need to be plugged into a power supply. It could be searched to look up specific information or access particular sections. And its per-unit cost would be low. At the end of the essay, he revealed that he was, in fact, describing a *book*, to demonstrate that with all these advantages, print media might be supplemented—but never replaced—by electronic media.

According to independent book publisher Dan Poynter, 80 percent of U.S. families did not buy or read a book last year, 70 percent of U.S. adults have not entered a bookstore in the last five years, and 58 percent of adults never read another book after high school.

On the other hand, notes Poynter, U.S. adults spent $25.6 billion on books in 1996—almost five times the $5.4 billion they spent going to the movies. "The pessimist says our market is smaller than we thought," Poynter tells book lovers. "The optimist says our potential market is larger than we thought."

And what about the World Wide Web, on-line content, and electronic publishing? Some people are cheering them, saying that they are the next step in the evolution of the printed word as it moves from ink on paper to electrons on glass.

I'm not so sure. The fact that we, as a species, feel a need to have instantaneous access to gigabytes of data seems to signal a coarser, meaner, and less genteel world.

Novelist Umberto Eco, writing in *World Press Review*, disagrees with those who think that printed books will not endure. "The appearance of new means of information does not destroy earlier ones; it frees them from one kind of constraint or another," observes Eco, noting that painting and drawing did not die with the invention of photography and cinema. He says that of the two types of books—reference books versus books meant to be read—only the former are likely to be replaced by the Internet and CD-ROMs.

"There is no doubt that the new media will eliminate the books in the first category," writes Eco. "Today, you can have the entire *Encyclopedia Britannica* on CD-ROM or access it on the Internet for very little money. We will save a lot of paper, and will preserve trees."

"But we cannot get rid of books that we sit down to read—from *The Iliad* to the latest novel," Eco says. "Reading them cover-to-cover on the screen would be tiring." Eco agrees with Asimov that the book is one of those inventions (like the hammer, spoon, and fork) for which no better ergonomic substitute has been found. "The book fits well in the hand, and one can read it in almost any situation, including in bed."

So, my kids can escape the pressures of life with video games or by watching TV. As for me, I'd rather curl up with a good book and read as the world passes me by.

BUMPER STICKERS

~

THERE'S AN OLD SAYING, "IF YOU CAN'T FIT YOUR IDEA on the back of a business card, you don't have a good idea." In the same way, if you can't express your philosophy or sentiment on a bumper sticker, you can't explain it clearly.

In her book *Bumper Sticker Wisdom*, Carol Gardner calls bumper stickers "America's pulpit above the tailpipe." But it's a pulpit where the lay preacher is king—anyone can buy a bumper sticker for a dollar, stick it on the back of his or her car, and express an opinion to thousands of fellow motorists.

There are some 183 million motor vehicles registered in the United States. Estimating conservatively that 10 percent of them carry bumper stickers, this would mean that 18 million vehicles carry bumper stickers, conclude Michael and Dawn Reilly in their book *The Bumper Sticker Book*.

I collect bumper sticker slogans as a hobby, the way other people collect state quarters or Italian stamps. Some of the recent goodies I've gotten include:

- *If God wanted me to cook and clean, I'd have been born with stainless-steel hands.*

- *My boss is a Jewish carpenter.*

- *It's not how you pick your nose, it's where you put the boogers.*

- *My child can beat up your honor student.*

- *The more you complain, the longer God lets you live.*

- *Sorry, I brake for red lights.*

- *Old age and treachery will overcome youth and skill.*

- *If you can read this, you're too close. I can stop and my lawyer can sue.*

- *I tried to contain myself, but I escaped.*

- *Ginger Rogers did everything Fred Astaire did, only backwards and in high heels!*

I created a bumper sticker that reads, "Everything I need to know I learned from bumper stickers." I will send you one free if you send me a bumper sticker slogan for my collection! If you don't have a slogan to send me and still want my bumper sticker, just send me $1 and a self-addressed, stamped envelope: Bob Bly, 22 E. Quackenbush Avenue, Dumont, NJ 07628.

Bumper stickers are a symbol of perhaps the greatest blessing we Americans enjoy, freedom of speech. Let me close with a few of the most recent gems that have come to my mailbox from around the country:

- *Those who plan to seek God at the 11th hour die at 10:30.*

- *If you object to logging, try using plastic toilet paper.*

- *Friends are like angels. They help you learn to use your wings when you've forgotten how.*

- *I'm dressed, I'm out of the house—what more do you want?*

- *Be alert. America needs more lerts.*

- *I love cats. They taste just like chicken.*

- *If you can read this, thank a teacher.*

- *Don't be caught dead without Jesus.*

- *If you don't like the way I drive, stay off the sidewalk.*

- *Love is a gift that grows only when you give it away.*

- *Age is a number and mine is unlisted.*

- *Thank you for holding your breath while I smoke.*

- *Grow your own dope . . . plant a man.*

- *God, help me remember: Nothing will happen to me today that you and I can't handle.*

CDs

~

SINCE, AS A RULE, I HATE GADGETS, I AM ALWAYS THE last person on the block to adopt a new technology. For instance, I don't have a Palm Pilot, laptop computer, or even a cell phone.

Based on this reluctance to jump into new things, I refused to replace my trusty record player with a CD player, and so for years I never bought CDs. But a couple of years ago, I got a free CD player as a prize, and now I'm a regular CD of the Month club member.

I used to listen to music mostly in the car, where I had a superior audiotape sound system. Problem was, I would leave tapes on the seat and dashboard, and on hot days the sun would melt them into odd shapes that wouldn't fit in the player.

Unlike tapes, CDs don't melt. And unlike records, they don't warp or scratch.

CDs aren't glitch-proof; sometimes a CD will start to skip and stall. But that's because the surface got dirty, and you can fix it easily with a tissue and some Windex.

Records and tapes had limited run times, but CDs have a far greater storage capacity. This has prompted music publishers to toss in an extra track or two when reissuing a record as a CD, so I'm getting more music for my money.

Also, wear and tear on tapes and records eventually caused the sound quality on certain portions to deteriorate, but so far, my CDs have shown themselves immune to this syndrome. That means what comes out of the sound system sounds better.

And with CDs, a push of a button takes you instantly to the song you want. No more bouncing around a record album with a needle, or going back and forth with the forward and reverse buttons on a cassette tape to find the right track.

P.S. I still have an eight-track tape player stored in my mother's basement. Now, if I could only get some eight-track tapes to play on it . . .

CHEMISTRY SETS

~

CAN YOU IMAGINE MAKING A CAREER CHOICE BASED on a horror movie or a toy? Well, I did both.

As a child in the 1960s, I was blissfully unaware of hippie protests. My consciousness was focused with laser-like intensity on comic books, science fiction, horror movies, and—above all else—my chemistry set.

Science was my favorite subject in school, but it was the laboratory scenes in the horror and science-fiction movies that intensified my desire to have a lab of my own.

I started with a Gilbert chemistry set, lovingly setting up the test tubes and numbered bottles of chemicals on a work-table in the basement of my parents' home. It was the first home my parents owned, having recently moved from a rented first-floor apartment in a two-family house; and as we looked at potential new homes to buy, my one request was that the house have a room for my "laboratory."

My mother, who had been a chemistry major before turning to psychology, understood my lab love and took me to a wholesale scientific supply house from time to time. At the counter, I would gleefully spend my small allowance on beakers, flasks, and graduated cylinders to expand my lab far beyond what Gilbert thought was necessary for a prepubescent chemist.

In retrospect, perhaps my mother was too liberal in what she permitted me to add to the lab. Since I had no Bunsen burner, she allowed me to buy a portable blowtorch, which I kept on my lab table in a makeshift stand I formed out of a wire coat hanger.

She also let me buy a bottle of sulfuric acid, a powerful reagent that a ten-year-old has no business handling. I poured the acid into a container of sugar and watched the sweet white granules transform into a single hard, black lump resembling coal.

Despite her own chemical bent, my mother was not always pleased by the results of my experiments. Her least favorite was when I distilled wood by heating wood splinters in a test tube. I did it to create the stinky tarlike substance, which I thought had strong practical-joke potential (but never had the nerve to actually use). But the distillation also produced a stinky yellow gas, the odor of which lingered in my basement lab—which doubled as my mother's laundry room—for many days. She reminded me by exclaiming "Oh, *phew!*" loudly every time she went down the basement steps carrying a load of (and she was very specific about this) *my* laundry.

My love for chemistry intensified in high school, where in Mr. Oliver's class I got an A+ by building a working model of a voltaic pile and producing electricity. I also put my sulfuric acid to work again building a lead storage battery.

But when I entered the University of Rochester as a chemistry major, I got a rude awakening: It takes a lot more than tinkering with a chemistry set today to be a good chemist.

This wasn't always the case. Hundreds of years ago, many important discoveries in chemistry were made by amateurs who, like me, simply enjoyed playing with chemicals and chemical equipment. Joseph Priestley, for example, a Unitarian minister who was an amateur chemist on the side, discovered oxygen by burning chemicals with a magnifying glass, the same kind of magnifying glass kids use to ignite leaves and paper on summer days.

Like me, Priestley also had a fondness for sulfuric acid. He dropped chalk into a flask of acid, collected the gas, and bubbled the carbon dioxide into a beaker, creating the world's first glass of club soda.

But modern chemistry requires a broader range of skills than just puttering around the lab. These include the manipulation of chemical formulas, calculus, and computer programming. I switched my major to chemical engineering, for which I had even less of an aptitude.

I barely escaped college with my bachelor's degree in chemical engineering, a profession for which I was wholly unsuited. Does this mean my years of playing with chemistry sets and my chemical education were wasted?

Quite the contrary. As a freelance writer, my background in science and engineering gives me a broad base of knowledge I apply every day—especially in a society as technology driven as ours. I even started a Web site for people interested in chemistry and playing with chemistry sets (www.mychemset.com).

Do I still play with a chemistry set? I thought that phase of my life was over, but another surprise—this one happy—intervened. I have two sons, and my youngest, Stephen, eight, has inherited my scientific interests. We have already used up the supplies in two beginner's chemistry sets and are setting up a space for a more extensive laboratory in the basement.

I wish I could give Stephen my old lab equipment. But years before he was born, because the garage was cluttered, I wrapped the beakers, flasks, and graduated cylinders in old newspapers and gave them to a friend's teenage child, and the gear is long gone.

So Steve and I will have to go to the lab equipment supplier and start assembling our laboratory from scratch. But we don't mind. In fact, that's half the fun.

CLIENTS AND CUSTOMERS

~

A FRIEND WHO IS SELF-EMPLOYED AS A GRAPHIC ARTIST told me he was having a bad day—so terrible, in fact, that he was contemplating giving up his freelance career for a nine-to-five job.

Was he sick of graphic design? No, he said, he still liked doing the work, but the people were driving him crazy. "This would be a great business if it weren't for the clients," he commented grimly.

Wrong. If it weren't for the clients and customers, you and I and everyone else in business would be *out* of business. In fact, pleasing customers is the sole reason our companies (whether we own them or are employed by someone else) exist.

Can people be difficult to deal with? Absolutely. Can customers give us grief? Of course. But our prosperity depends on satisfying enough customers often enough to keep us in business.

One thing that has helped me is to realize that people don't *mean* to be mean. They're not intentionally difficult or rude. It's just that folks are so busy, and have so much to do, that when there is a problem or delay, they blow their stack.

Put yourself in the customer's shoes. If your car wasn't ready when it was supposed to be . . . if the steak was rare instead of well-done as you requested . . . would you be upset? Well, then don't be shocked when your customers complain. After all, they're only human.

I know lots of people who say, "I hate clients." Well, I love my clients! They give me the opportunity to do the work I enjoy and earn a living so I can take care of my family. Without customers, you don't *have* a business.

In his best-selling book, *Think and Grow Rich*, Napoleon Hill said that "a positive mental attitude" and "a pleasing personality" are the two most effective tools for dealing effectively with people in business. They will make customers happy. And when your customers are happy, you reap the rewards.

COLOR

~

IF YOU'VE EVER DECORATED OR FURNISHED A NEW home, you know how important color is to you as a consumer—you want everything to match precisely. But in addition to its aesthetic value, color plays other important roles in our lives. Numerous studies show that color affects human emotion and mood. In addition, color communicates in an almost universal language—for instance, yellow is bright and cheerful to people all over the world. Yet, a system for communicating color specifications in design, art, and business did not exist until the twentieth century.

No one "invented" color. Well, God did. But, in 1905, Professor Albert H. Munsell brought clarity to color communication by establishing an orderly system for accurately identifying every color that exists: the Munsell Color System. He founded the Munsell Color Company in 1918 to produce physical color standards in the form of paper swatches. Today the Munsell system is the universal method for selecting, specifying, and controlling color—in short, the universal language of color communication.

The Munsell Color System is a way of precisely specifying colors in written form. What is "bright red" to me may create an entirely different image in your mind. Prior to

Munsell, the only way to communicate color was to look at an actual sample or swatch.

What Munsell did was to invent a notation that allows color to be communicated in written form. This way, a buyer can communicate to her supplier the exact color she wants for those new curtains, either over the phone or in a letter or e-mail, without physically obtaining a color sample and shipping it to the supplier.

In the Munsell Color system, every color has three qualities or attributes: hue, value, and chroma. These attributes are given the symbols H, V, and C and are written in a form HV/C, which is called the "Munsell notation."

Hue refers to the basic color as it appears in a spectrum or rainbow: red, yellow, green, and blue. There is a natural order of hues, or colors.

The colors in a rainbow, for example, always appear in the same order. (In elementary school you may have learned the pneumonic "Roy G. Biv" to help you remember the rainbow colors and their order—red, orange, yellow, green, blue, indigo, violet).

Paints can be mixed to obtain different variations in hue. Red and yellow may be mixed in any proportion to obtain all the hues from red through orange to yellow. The same is true for yellow and green, green and blue, blue and purple, and purple and red.

Value indicates the lightness of a color. The lower the value, the darker the color. The scale of value ranges from 0 for pure black to 10 for pure white.

Black, white, and the grays between them are called "neutral colors." They have no hue. Colors that have a hue are called "chromatic colors."

Chroma is the degree of departure of a color from the neutral color of the same value. Colors of low chroma are sometimes called "weak," and have a washed-out appearance. Colors of high chroma are said to be "highly saturated," "strong," or "vivid." They appear . . . well . . . colorful.

Imagine mixing a little vivid yellow paint with a gray paint of the same value. If you started with gray and gradually added increasing proportions of yellow until the original vivid yellow color was obtained, you would develop a series of gradually changing colors that increase in chroma. On the other hand, if you started with pure vivid yellow and added more and more gray, you would be decreasing the chroma.

In the Munsell notation, colors are specified symbolically as HV/C. For a vivid red having a hue of 5R, a value of 6 and a chroma of 14, the complete notation is 5R 6/14. When a finer division is needed for any of the attributes, decimals are used. For example, 5.3R 6.1/14.4.

Most of us think of color as a simple matter—like choosing the right colors from a box of crayons—but actually it is much more complicated than that. Munsell is generally recognized as one of the founders of modern color science.

Most of the world's commerce today, especially products dependent on brand marketing, is visually driven by color—for instance, the trademark red on Coca Cola cans and bottles, or the vivid blue of Blue Cross and Blue Shield. In fact, large corporations are beginning to patent the unique color blends created for their logos and packaging materials.

Another interesting fact: Without light, color does not exist! According to the book *Fundamentals of Color and Appearance* (GretagMacbeth), color is not a thing that exists independent of the viewer; it is a "psychophysical response." The phenomenon of color results from the physical interaction of light energy with an object, and the subjective experience of an individual observer.

Without light, there is no color. Conversely, if you see color, there must be light. So anytime you see cheerful colors, it's literally a bright spot in your day!

COMPOUND INTEREST

~

WE USED TO DEFINE A TRULY WEALTHY PERSON BY saying, "He/she is a millionaire." But a million dollars doesn't buy what it used to. Now financial planners tell us we need a million dollars just to retire comfortably!

It sounds out of reach, but thanks to compound interest, it isn't. Investments earn annual returns ranging from 1 to 25 percent and sometimes much more. Naturally, the longer you hold an investment and it earns a return, the more its value increases.

But thanks to compound interest, the increase in value is not merely linear; it's almost exponential. Therefore, when you start early, your investments will grow in value much more spectacularly than someone who gets a late start. In his book *Money Doesn't Grow on Trees*, investment counselor Mark Dutton says, "Compound interest is the eighth wonder of the world."

And with this comes a warning: If you don't start now, you'll lose out. The most important thing you can do to assure a healthy financial future is to start at twenty instead of thirty, or if you're thirty, to start at thirty instead of waiting until forty.

If you start late, you lose ten years of compound interest—a ten-year start on building your wealth. The total you end up with will decline enormously. And once you let those early years go, you can never reclaim them; the "magic" of the compound interest is lost forever.

For instance, Merrill Lynch says that a person who puts $2,000 a year in an IRA starting at age eighteen will retire with more than double the savings of a person who starts only ten years later, at age twenty-eight.

Wayne Kolb, CPA, had an even more dramatic example in his *Tax Planning* newsletter (June 1995). Let's say an eighteen-year-old invests $2,000 annually in an IRA up to age twenty-five, with an annual return average of 10 percent, and then stops. By age sixty-five, his IRA will be worth more than $1 million! Not a bad return for a $16,000 investment.

In comparison, if a person waits until age twenty-five to start an IRA, as I did, he or she will need to invest $2,000 a year until retirement to have $1 million. Two thousand dollars a year for forty years, from age twenty-five to sixty-five, is $80,000—meaning the person who started his IRA seven years later, at age twenty-five instead of eighteen, had to put in five times the investment of the person who started earlier.

But whatever your age when you read this, if you haven't started investing in earnest, the best advice I can give is: do so now. Not in a week, but now. An example from Prudential Securities dramatizes this point: If you open an IRA at age fifty, and contribute $2,000 a year earning 8 percent compounded monthly, at age 65 your IRA will be worth $54,300.

Had you opened the same IRA when you were twenty-five,

and put in the same amount of money annually earning the same rate of return, at age sixty-five your IRA would be worth more than half a million dollars—almost ten times as much.

It is never too late to start investing, but the earlier you start, the better off you will be in your later years. If you are pooh-poohing my notion of socking away money now, keep these sobering facts in mind:

- Because Americans are not savers, the median total net worth of families with parents between ages thirty-five to fourty-five is only $35,000. Their share of the national debt, by comparison, is $78,000 per family.

- More than half of all wage earners become dependent on their families, pensions, the community, or social security to live in their old age. Yet according to Prudential Securities, social security and employer-sponsored pension plans provide only 59 percent of aggregate retirement income.

- Only 5 percent of the population retires financially independent and in relative comfort.

The best financial advice I ever received was, "Live *below* your means." Do not build debt by acquiring so many possessions that decrease in value. Invest in assets that appreciate in value and produce income. Collect interest rather than pay it.

CONFIDENCE

~

DON'T EVER LET ANYONE TELL YOU THAT THERE'S anything wrong with self-congratulation. When you've done something hard, you deserve cheers, from yourself and everyone around you. When you've done something hard and it's worked, you deserve a banquet! You may remember that when you were setting your goal, I told you that you would need to be able to know beyond a doubt when you had arrived—at your goal and at each big step on the way. I can tell you now that part of the reason was so you would know when to celebrate.

Pausing to savor your own accomplishments and feel proud of yourself isn't "conceited" or "self-indulgent" the way our Puritan culture taught us it was. It's food for your unfolding self. And you don't need to worry about "resting on your laurels." You've got to rest on them a little bit, if only to catch your breath! Then you'll want to move on. So enjoy this moment of triumph, in private and with the people you love.

—BARBARA SHER, *WISHCRAFT*, BALLANTINE BOOKS

I envy people who have a lot of self-confidence. Life seems easier for them—and less fearsome.

I am the opposite. I suffer from low self-confidence and low self-esteem.

My coping mechanism for this is a finely developed sense of self-effacing humor.

For instance, I've put on a little too much weight lately. I'm not obese, but I could stand to go on the diet my fellow Thomas Nelson author Dr. Don Colbert recommends in his book *What Would Jesus Eat?*

Recently I appeared as a guest on a local TV talk show. "You did so well!" my assistant gushed. But all I could see was a blimp on camera.

A client called to congratulate me on the appearance.

"You know how they say the camera adds ten pounds?" I asked him.

"Yes," he said, sensing that I knew that *he* knew I had put on weight.

"Well," I replied, "there were six cameras in that studio!"

I envy people with strong self-confidence. People like celebrities, captains of industry, and leaders of nations, for example.

They seem to believe their works, ideas, and words are right and true and superior. And through this belief and enthusiasm, they are able to convince others of the same. Therefore their beliefs become popular, their products get bought, and their principles gain a large following.

If you possess a healthy degree of self-confidence, God bless you. Make the most of it.

If you're in my camp, think better of yourself. Have more confidence in your ideas and abilities. Remember the old saying: If you think you can, you will. If you think you can't, you probably won't. Self-confidence isn't everything, but it's close.

CREATIVITY

~

At an evening party, Mozart bet Haydn a case of champagne that the older man could not play at sight a piece he had composed that afternoon. Haydn accepted the bet, the piece was placed on the spinet rack, and Haydn briskly played the first few bars, then stopped short. He found it impossible to continue, for the composition prescribed playing with the two hands at the two ends of the keyboard and striking a note in the very center. Haydn confessed himself beaten. Mozart took his place at the piano and, reaching the fatal note, bent forward and hit it with his nose.

—Clifton Fadiman, *The Little, Brown Book of Anecdotes*, Little, Brown and Company

You're creative. That's right, you! And I can prove it.

Many people mistakenly believe that creativity only applies to the arts, like painting, music, and poetry. Not true. Creativity is simply the ability to have ideas. And everyone has them. All the time.

You're already a creative person. You have ideas all the time. But to help you maximize your creative powers, it helps to know the process by which you generate ideas. You already follow it subconsciously, perhaps without having identified the individual steps. But here is the creative process laid out step-by-step. Make sure you practice these steps in your thinking, and you'll rarely be stuck for another creative idea again.

The steps, in order: Identify the problem, assemble pertinent facts, gather general knowledge, look for combinations, sleep on it, use a checklist, get feedback, team up, and give new ideas a chance.

1. *Identify the problem.* The first step in solving a problem is to know what the problem is. But many of us forge ahead without knowing what we are trying to accomplish. Moral: Don't apply a solution before you have taken the time to accurately define the problem.

2. *Assemble pertinent facts.* In crime stories, detectives spend most of their time looking for clues. They cannot solve a case with clever thinking alone; they must have the facts. You, too, must have the facts before you can solve a problem or make an informed decision.

3. *Gather general knowledge.* Specific facts have to do with the project at hand. They include the budget, the schedule, the resources available, the customer's specifications, plus knowledge of the products, components, and techniques to be used in completing the project. General knowledge has to do with the expertise you've developed, and includes your storehouse of information about life, events, people, science, technology, management, and the world at large.

Become a student in the many areas that relate to your

job. In most industries, trade journals are the most valuable source of general knowledge. Subscribe to the journals that relate to your field. Scan them all, and clip and save articles containing information that may be useful to you. Organize your clip files for easy access to articles by subject. Read books in your field and start a reference library.

Most of the successful professionals I know are compulsive information collectors. You should be too.

4. *Look for combinations.* Someone once complained to me, "There's nothing new in the world. It's all been done before." Maybe. But an idea doesn't have to be something completely new. Many ideas are simply a new combination of existing elements. By looking for combinations, for new relationships between old ideas, you can come up with a fresh approach.

The clock radio, for example, was invented by someone who combined two existing technologies—the clock and the radio. Niels Bohr combined two separate ideas— Rutherford's model of the atom as a nucleus orbited by electrons and Planck's quantum theory—to create the modern conception of the atom.

Look for synergistic combinations when you examine the facts. What two things can work together to form a third thing that is a new idea? If you have two devices, and each performs a function you need, can you link them together to create a new invention?

5. *Sleep on it.* Putting the problem aside for a time can

help you renew your idea-producing powers just when you think your creative well has run dry.

But don't resort to this method after only five minutes of puzzled thought. First, you must gather all the information you can. Next, you need to go over the information again and again as you try to come up with that one big idea. You'll come to a point where you get bleary and punch-drunk, just hashing the same ideas over and over. This is the time to take a break, to put the problem aside, to sleep on it and let your unconscious mind take over.

A solution may strike you as you sleep, shower, shave, or walk in the park. Even if it doesn't, when you return to the problem, you will find you can attack it with renewed vigor and a fresh perspective. I use this technique in writing—I put aside what I have written and read it fresh the next day. Many times the things that I thought were brilliant when I wrote them can be much improved at second glance.

6. *Use a checklist.* Checklists can be used to stimulate creative thinking and as a starting point for new ideas. Many manufacturers, consultants, technical magazines, and trade associations publish checklists you can use in your own work. But the best checklists are those you create yourself, because they are tailored to the problems that come up in your daily routine.

However, no checklist can contain an idea for every situation that comes up. Remember, a checklist should be used as a tool for creative thinking, not as a crutch.

7. *Get feedback*. Sherlock Holmes was a brilliant detective. But even he needed to bounce ideas off Dr. Watson at times. As a professional writer, I think I know how to write an engaging piece of copy. But when I show a draft to my wife, she can always spot at least half a dozen ways to make it better.

Some people prefer to work alone. I'm one of them, and maybe you are too. But even if you don't work as part of a team, getting someone else's opinion of your work can help you focus your thinking and produce ideas you hadn't thought of.

Consider the feedback for what it's worth. If you feel you are right, and the criticisms are off base, ignore them. But more often than not, feedback will provide useful information that can help you come up with the best, most profitable ideas.

8. *Team up*. Some people think more creatively when working in groups. But how large should the group be? In my opinion, two is the ideal team. Any more and you're in danger of ending up with a committee that spins its wheels and accomplishes nothing. The person you team up with should have skills and thought processes that balance and complement your own. For example, in advertising, copywriters (the word people) team up with art directors (the picture people).

In entrepreneurial firms, the idea person who started the company will often hire a professional manager from one of the Fortune 500 companies as the new venture grows; the entrepreneur knows how to make things happen, but the manager knows how to run a profitable, efficient corporation.

9. *Give new ideas a chance.* Many businesspeople, especially managers, develop their critical faculties more finely than their creative faculties. If creative engineers and inventors had listened to these people, we would not have personal computers, cars, airplanes, light bulbs, or electricity.

The creative process works in two stages. The first is the idea-producing stage, when ideas flow freely. The second is the critical or "editing" stage, when you hold each idea up to the cold light of day and see if it is practical.

Many of us make the mistake of mixing the stages together. During the idea-producing stage, we are too eager to criticize an idea as soon as it is presented. As a result, we shoot down ideas and make snap judgments when we should instead be encouraging the production of ideas. And many good ideas are killed this way.

Every individual has powers of creativity and imagination. But our lives are unique; only you have lived your life. Combined, your creative powers and your unique base of experience enable you to come up with ideas no one else has thought of before.

So don't underestimate yourself in the creativity department. You're an original. We all are.

DEMOCRACY

(And the fact that anyone can run for, and be elected to,
any office in the land—from the board of education
to the presidency of the United States)

~

IN OUR WONDERFUL DEMOCRATIC SOCIETY, ALMOST
anybody (ex-convicts and minors excepted) can become president. But few people know how.

In case political office—from the presidency down to the
board of education—is your ambition, I am providing, as a
public service, the proven formula that successful candidates
use to get themselves elected.

According to this formula, there are four attributes each
candidate has in varying amounts. A successful campaign
will convince voters that one candidate is the right choice
because he has these attributes: (1) past performance, (2)
future promise, (3) credibility, and (4) ideology.

1. Past performance. What has the candidate done for voters in the past, either in government service, business, or
other capacities? One way to demonstrate good past performance is by citing a specific track record; for example, the
candidate voted against tax hikes for property owners three
times.

Another method is to imply that generally good conditions in the candidate's voting district are largely a result of

his or her being in office. For instance, former president Bill Clinton enjoyed a high performance rating due to the good economy, and voters are not asking for proof he directly created those conditions.

2. *Future promise.* Past performance is, "What have you done for me?" Future promise is, "What will you do for me if I elect you?" Sometimes this future promise is a platform of intended actions. In other campaigns, it can hinge mainly on how the candidate says he or she will act regarding a key issue (for example, attacking fraud).

3. *Credibility.* Credibility is, "Who is this person? Should I trust him or her? Should I believe he or she will do what he or she says?" Credibility can be created many ways.

Dwight Eisenhower stressed experience as a successful general in World War II to create a rugged war-hero image, in contrast with Adlai Stevenson's intellectual-liberal label.

Ross Perot and Steve Forbes have made the analogy that they are successful at running businesses; therefore they could do the same with the federal government.

Factors that tie the candidate to his or her constituency also work well in building credibility and connections with voters. If you are running for office in Florida, for example, and your children and grandchildren live in the state, saying so builds your image as a Florida family man or woman.

4. *Ideology.* Ideology is, "What is your belief system?" Are you conservative or liberal? Democrat or Republican? Libertarian or socialist? Believe in big or minimal government?

The important point is that a candidate need not possess each attribute in equal measure to win. Think of these four attributes as four legs of a stool (this analogy comes from expert advertising executive Michael Masterson).

A stool with four legs can stand even if one leg is missing, or if two legs are weak. Likewise, a politician can be weak on past performance (for example, someone entering politics for the first time) and still win if his credibility and current platform are strong.

In a democracy, any citizen can run for public office and be elected in the service of others. Have you taken advantage of this opportunity?

DOGS

~

MY FATHER DIDN'T LIKE DOGS. BUT WHEN I WAS TEN, my sister and I begged for a dog so much that we wore him down. He bought us Heidi, a tricolor collie puppy.

Heidi grew to be huge and clumsy. She knocked over lamps, chewed tables, and occasionally threw up or pooped on the carpet.

Within a year, my father had enough. He then did the only thing in my life I really resented him doing: He gave Heidi away to another family.

Although I was a passionate dog lover as a child, as an adult, I am closer to my father. Overwork, a busy life, and family pressures leave me little time or energy to fuss over a dog. We own one, a sheltie named Brownie, and I love him; but he is more my kids' dog than mine.

Nevertheless, dogs have qualities that make them great pets: They are loving, loyal, sweet, affectionate, and fun. For adults who remain unmarried or childless, a dog can be a constant companion and an important source of love. Hudson, my sister's dog, is a much more important part of her life than Brownie is of mine. Same goes for Max, my brother-in-law's dog.

Just reading this over makes me more appreciative of having a loving pet. I think I'll stop now and go play with Brownie.

EARS

(And the ability to hear and listen)

~

IT'S NOT THE GIFT OF THE GAB YOU NEED, IT'S THE gift of the earhole. Machiavelli said knowledge is power, and power is what we are after—the power to change the future, to bring about our desired outcome without fail. If you're talking, you're giving information and therefore giving away power; if you're listening and asking questions, you're gaining information, the raw material of knowledge, and therefore gaining power.

—GEOFF BURCH, *RESISTANCE IS USELESS*, HEADLINE

A writing teacher I know says to avoid clichés in writing, but the reason so many sayings became clichés is because of the truth they contain.

A good example is: "God gave us two ears but only one mouth, so we should listen twice as much as we talk."

Sounds corny, but it is absolutely true. Whenever I spend most of the time listening, I am successful, whether in business or parenting or buying a car. When I do most of the talking—because I am in a hurry, impatient, or think what I want to say is so important—I invariably lose.

Amazingly, though listening is a simple process and one of the main ways we learn, this skill is not taught in schools.

The process of listening follows this sequence:

1. *Hearing.* The first step is to simply pay attention to make sure you've heard the message. If your boss says, "McGillicudy, I need the report on last month's sales," and you can repeat the sentence, then you have heard her.

2. *Interpretation.* Failure to correctly interpret the speaker's words frequently leads to misunderstanding. People sometimes interpret words differently because of varying experience, knowledge, vocabulary, culture, background, and attitudes.

A good speaker uses tone of voice, facial expressions, and mannerisms to help make the message clear to the listener. For instance, if your boss speaks loudly, frowns, and puts her hands on her hips, you know she is probably upset and angry.

3. *Evaluation.* During the third step, evaluation, you decide what to do with the information you have received. For example, when listening to a sales pitch, you have two options: You choose either to believe or to disbelieve the salesperson. The judgments you make in the evaluation stage are a crucial part of the listening process.

4. *Response.* The final step is to respond to what you have heard. This is a verbal or visual response that lets the speaker know whether you have gotten the message and what your reaction is.

When you listen, you understand. When you understand, you communicate. And here's the hidden benefit of listening: When other people see that you are listening to them, they will listen to you.

ELECTRICITY

~

You walk into your house at night, flip a switch, and are bathed in the warm glow of electric lights. We all take electricity for granted, but if the imminent global energy crisis comes to pass, we won't be able to for much longer.

Demand for electricity in the United States is growing at breakneck speed. Electricity is being used to power everything from millions of Internet appliances and PCs to cars and cell phones.

The result is a massive boom in electricity. In the last twenty years, consumption of electricity has more than doubled—with demand far outstripping the supply. In the next twenty years, U.S. electricity consumption is expected to rise almost 30 percent more.

Utilities simply cannot keep up with consumption. In California, for instance, the Bonneville Power Administration says that California can no longer rely on electricity from twenty-nine hydroelectric dams in four Northwestern states to make up for the shortfall from California's in-state plants. (California imports nearly 30 percent of its total power from other states in the Pacific Northwest.)

The total cost for power in California quadrupled from $7 billion in 1999 to $28 billion in 2000—a fourfold increase in just one year! Estimates put California's energy costs for 2001 in the $50 billion range.

During the latest California energy shortfall, businesses lost between $70,000 and $6 million per hour during every power brownout or blackout. High-tech firms that suffered a three-hour power outage in June 2000 lost as much as $1 million per hour.

Similarly, Con Ed in New York City says it can't keep the electricity flowing if next summer is as hot as the last one.

The "utility grid" is overtaxed beyond its capacity. Existing power plants, many of them decades old, are already at maximum capacity. There's no way to get the grid to meet the growing demand, which is why we're seeing blackouts and brownouts throughout the country during peak summer demand periods.

U.S. Secretary of Energy Spencer Abraham concludes: "My assessment is that we have an energy crisis. It's a long-term crisis . . . we certainly are confronting the greatest challenge we've had in at least two decades."

But just as Thomas Edison's genius brought us into the electric age with the invention of the light bulb in 1886, today clever scientists are solving today's energy crisis.

For example, solar power has been around a long time. Our sun converts 4 million tons of hydrogen to helium per second through nuclear fusion. Even though we are 93 million miles from the sun, the Earth receives about 85 trillion kilowatts of constant energy from sunlight—equivalent to the energy that would come from burning 1,150 billion tons of coal per year.

The problem has been that solar power costs too much because of the inefficiency of the solar cells that convert the sun's rays to usable energy.

Years ago, solar energy cost more than $500 per kilowatt-hour (kWh). But thanks to recent research breakthroughs, increased efficiency in solar collection systems has reduced the cost of solar energy one hundredfold to around $5 per kilowatt-hour.

By comparison, in 1999 the average cost per kilowatt-hour for electricity from natural gas-fired power plants was $3.52, and for oil, $3.18 per kWh.

That means for the first time ever, solar power is becoming cost-competitive with utility power.

Soon we will have a rich variety of alternative energy sources—solar, wind, geothermal, hydrogen fuel cells—to make up the shortfall from the utilities. And our energy problems will be solved.

Every time you plug in your toaster and it makes toast, it's a small miracle you take for granted. Appreciate the miracle.

ETHICS

~

EVEN WHEN WE LIVE BENEVOLENT, ADMIRED LIVES
according to the standards of our times, we can fear that
had things been tougher we would have joined the fallen.
If we are good, it may be because we were never tempted
enough, or frightened enough, or put in desperate
enough need.

—SIMON BLACKBURN, *BEING GOOD*,
OXFORD UNIVERSITY PRESS

Ethics, or rather the sense of ethics implanted in the
human psyche, are what permit us to live in comfort and relative security in a peaceful society. Without ethics, there
would be chaos. Agreement could not be made, personal
relationships would fall apart, contracts would be meaning-
less, financial markets could not operate, and services and
goods could not be purchased.

What are ethics? Ethics are the rules or standards for
moral behavior. *Moral* means that society as a whole finds
the behaviors acceptable, permissible, and even desirable.
Ethical behavior, then, is living and acting in conformance
with morality. Samuel Butler (1835–1902) defined *morality*
as "the custom of one's country and the current feeling of
one's peers."

Ayn Rand comments: "That which is proper to the life of a rational being is the good; that which negates, opposes, or destroys it is the evil." Richard J. Leider, in his book *The Power of Purpose*, contends that—conveniently—individual needs and societal needs mesh: "Our needs as individuals uniquely match the needs or our organizations, our society, and our planet."

Why behave ethically? There are several reasons.

First, if you've ever been treated unethically, you know it was an unpleasant experience. People give as good as they get. Therefore, if you want people to behave ethically when dealing with you, you should behave ethically when dealing with them.

Second, your reputation is one of your most important assets. Good ethics maintain your reputation and enhance this asset.

Unethical behavior, on the other hand, can result in ill will and negative publicity that mar your reputation. This can cost you friends, relationships, business, or even your job.

Another reason to practice ethical behavior is to do so simply because it's *right*. For many of us, doing the right thing is important to our fundamental make-up as human beings, and so we strive to do right—although there may be many occasions when we are tempted to stray.

If you don't feel compelled or obligated to do right, the other two factors—encouraging decent treatment from others and protecting your reputation and good name—will have to provide sufficient motivation for you to adhere to ethical behavior.

In the business world, for instance, many workers these days feel tempted to do things that border on the illegal or the unethical. In one recent poll, 57 percent of workers surveyed felt more pressured now than five years ago to consider acting unethically or illegally on the job, and 40 percent said that pressure has increased over the last year.

According to a 1997 study sponsored by the Ethics Officer Association, 48 percent of employees admitted to illegal or unethical actions in 1996. In 1997, half of U.S. workers surveyed by the Ethics Officer Association said they used technology unethically on the job during the year, including copying company software for home use and wrongly blaming a personal error on a technology glitch.

In response, more and more organizations are training employees in ethics and establishing ethical guidelines for employees to follow. According to Harvard Business School Professor Joseph L. Badaracco Jr., one out of three American firms has ethics training programs, and more than five hundred have ethics officers. Six out of ten have ethical codes employees are supposed to follow. Lockheed Martin even has a toll-free "ethics hotline" its employees and suppliers can call to get advice on business-ethics issues. There are more than five hundred ethics courses offered at American business schools.

But it shouldn't take corporate training to make the practice of ethics widespread. Religious education instills a strong moral sense in youngsters; perhaps public schools should take a cue and teach courses in ethics in high school. And colleges should make it an undergraduate requirement.

Meanwhile, if we all taught ethics through example, we could make the world a much better place.

FAMILY

~

A SIX-YEAR-OLD BOY, SEPARATED FROM HIS MOTHER in a supermarket, began to call frantically for "Martha! Martha! Martha!"

That was his mother's name and she came running to him quickly. "But, honey," she admonished, "you shouldn't call me Martha. I'm 'Mother' to you."

"Yes, I know," he answered, "but this store is full of mothers, and I want mine."

—HERBERT V. PROCHNOW, *THE COMPLETE TOASTMASTER*, PRENTICE-HALL, INC.

You choose your friends and acquaintances and business associates. But you don't choose your family; you are thrown together by genetics and circumstance.

I think perhaps God created families so people would have other people who love and care for them no matter what their faults or what they do. There are some people almost everyone likes. There are other people almost no one likes. The institution of family ensures that everyone has someone to love, and someone to love them—which is perhaps the fundamental need we humans have aside from air, food, water, and shelter.

Does that mean some of us are "forced" to be the emotional

and financial caretakers of individuals with whom we otherwise might not even associate? Perhaps. But often the forced relationships add depth to our lives we might not otherwise have. An uncle I hardly knew when I was a child turned out to be a leader in the industry into which I went as an adult, and in later years we had an interesting and engaging relationship. A distant cousin, whom I also hardly knew, became a writer whose work I could admire and read with pleasure. A first cousin announced a transition into a career in which I had some experience, and we grew closer as I moved from "Cousin Bob" to career mentor.

In today's busy, fast-paced society, we increasingly have less time for family, and time and distance sever family bonds. We have close relatives we rarely see; some we never even talk with. Most we would find to be worthwhile people, if only we would invest the time to know them.

Eisenhower's speechwriter Joseph Kelley once said, "There is a kernel of interest in everything God created," and that includes people. If you are distant from your relatives, stop thinking of them as a necessary chore and start looking for the kernel of interest. You may find that Aunt Edith is more fascinating than any show on TV or any book in the library. And she has been aching for the attention from her family.

My father-in-law, Tom, has a special affinity for the elderly. He seeks out and builds relationships with older cousins who are often alone and do not have much contact with relatives spread out all over the country. Even though he is busy, he takes the time to make these cousins feel important and special. I think he's pretty special for doing so.

"One's family is the most important thing in life," said Robert C. Byrd. "I look at it this way: One of these days I'll be over in a hospital somewhere with four walls around me. And the only people who'll be with me will be my family."

FREEDOM

~

There are two nature-oriented fads popular in my area right now. One is bamboo shoots as houseplants.

The other is a houseplant with a live fish in the vase. My son Alex wanted one of these fish as a pet, and so we bought it. It's now on a table in my bedroom, and it's quite beautiful.

The plant sits in a clear plastic pot perched above a glass vase in which the fish, a Siamese fighting fish, swims. The roots of the plant dangle below the bottom of the pot and into the vase. Decorative blue gravel lines the bottom of the vase.

The setup is a type of biosphere. Have you seen the sealed aquariums where fish and plants coexist with no access to the outside atmosphere? The plants take in carbon dioxide and exhale oxygen; the fish breathe in oxygen and exhale carbon dioxide. The fish also eat the plants, which regenerate. The ecosystem is perfectly balanced, which is why the fish and plants can live in a sealed vessel for a year or longer.

The fish-in-a-vase is not quite as rigid as a sealed aquarium. The fish eats the roots, and theoretically doesn't need to be fed, but the sellers of these biosystems advise sprinkling in a little fish food now and then, which we do.

Other than that, there is none of the usual maintenance required with a traditional aquarium: no filter, no aeration, no daily feeding, and no monthly cleaning.

As I watch the fish, which Alex has named Aqua, swimming in his perfect environment, I notice how stress free his existence is, biologically speaking. He does not have to forage for food, cope with extremes of temperature, fend off predators, or fight for survival.

The vase isn't roomy, so Aqua doesn't actually swim much. He is motionless in the clear water most of the time, gently suspended in space.

He has security, peace, and serenity—things most of us often lack. But I wouldn't trade places with him for anything in the world, because he doesn't have the one thing so precious to humankind: freedom.

Aqua is trapped. He cannot leave the vase. He cannot move his habitat. He lives where we place him, eats what we feed him, and lives or dies at our whim.

The September 11, 2001, attacks on the United States have reminded us in a powerful way how precious our freedom is—how we take it for granted, how fleeting it is, how much we would fight to preserve it.

You can mostly go where you want to go, when you want to go there; do what you want to do, when you want to do it. It's commonplace. It's everyday. It's a miracle. It's unappreciated. Freedom may be the greatest gift we have.

Free Enterprise
(Entrepreneurship)

~

Winston Churchill once said, "Capitalism is the worst system of government in the world, except for everything else."

America is a nation of entrepreneurs, and I'm so grateful for that. I wasn't built for working for someone else, and being an American, I have more opportunities to avoid that life than I would if I lived anywhere else in the world.

Millions of Americans own their own businesses or are self-employed professionals. In this country, if you make a product or offer a service, chances are you can make a good living selling it to others.

I'm also one of those who favors less rather than more government, and that especially applies to small business. The less the government regulates and interferes with entrepreneurs, the better, in my opinion.

For instance, a recent government report says that, compared with a large corporation, the average small business has one hundred times the equivalent paperwork burden for taxes. A one- or two-person business cannot afford full-time staff just to handle government forms, as a big corporation can. Put too much administrative burden on small businesses, forcing them to fill out too many forms to comply with too many regulations, and soon they won't be able to afford to stay in business.

And in a country that is home to Col. Harland Sanders and Bill Gates and Lillian Vernon and Deborah Fields and Steve Jobs, that would be a crying shame.

FRIENDSHIP
~

PEOPLE WHO HAVE WARM FRIENDSHIPS ARE
healthier and happier than those who have none. A single
real friend is a treasure worth more than gold or precious
stones. Money can buy many things, good and evil. All
the wealth of the world could not buy you a friend or pay
you for the loss of one.

—C. D. PRENTICE, *THE HEART OF A FRIEND*,
PETER PAUPER PRESS

The people who make a difference in your life are not the
ones with the most credentials, the most money, or the
most awards. They are the ones who care.

—DR. ANDREW LINICK

Friendship is a weak area for me. As seems to be more
typically male than female, friends are not the critical part of
my life—work and family are.

I am a private, introverted person, and I do not cultivate
friendships. I don't spend much time with the few friends I
have. My father, at my age, had many friends he saw
weekly—at poker games, bowling, and other activities.

But working twelve hours a day, I don't have the time,
energy, or desire to participate in such activities. After work,

I exercise (not often enough), eat, and spend time with my kids. I spend what little time and energy remain reading or writing in my office.

My wife is the opposite. Her life is rich in friends, and she is, I believe, a happier, more balanced person for it.

We have discussed this. "I am a man, and most men, I think, get their self-esteem from work—how successful they are and how much money they make," I said.

"That's sad," Amy replied. "The most important things in my life are relationships—friends and family." Perhaps because of this, her life is filled with strong, meaningful friendships that bring her pleasure, comfort, and joy.

Are you like me, too busy for friends? My conclusion is that I am missing out on something. On the rare occasions that I spend some serious quality time with friends, I'm always surprised by how enjoyable it is—and how energized and invigorated I feel afterward. *Maybe I should do this more often,* I think. Maybe we all should.

GOD

~

THE GREATEST DISCOVERY IN MAN'S THINKING IS
that the world is good. The universe has goodness in its
heart and God is on the side of good. Existence is life with
a moral core. If you believe that God is good and that He
created a universe in which the devil can't win, then you
can live in peace and happiness.

—E. HOWARD CALLAHAN

If you believe in the Lord, He will do half the work—but
the last half. He helps those who help themselves.

—CYRUS H. K. CURTIS

I heard a great story the other day that beautifully illustrates
the well-known saying, "God helps those who help themselves."

A minister walking in a rock-strewn desert came upon a
house with the most beautiful, lush garden he had ever seen.
Wanting to make sure the owner appreciated God's handi-
work, he knocked on the door. The man opened it and
greeted the minister.

"Brother, do you see the miracle the Lord hath wrought?"
the minister began in his best Sunday-sermon voice. He
went on to praise the miracle of the garden in the desert at
considerable length.

"I appreciate what you say and it is all true. God has granted me a miracle," the man replied. "But . . . you should have seen what He had done with the place *before* I got here!"

Now you may be thinking, *This saying isn't in the Bible.* True, but the Bible does say that faith without works is dead, and it also teaches that those who can work but refuse to are in for trouble. So I don't think we miss the mark when we say, "God helps those who help themselves."

Good Manners

~

THE PLAIN TRUTH IS, YOU AND I ARE LIVING IN A
time when the distinction between right and wrong is
more blurred than at any time I can remember. Somehow
along the line, we have lost something as a culture . . .
somehow in these times we've forgotten that there are
limits to what kind of language and behavior are acceptable in a civil society, and what kind of responsibility our
role models have to those who are younger and more
impressionable than they are.

—SISTER MARY ROSE, COVENANT HOUSE,
WWW.COVENANTHOUSE.ORG

A bumper sticker I saw recently highlights the decline of
good manners in America: "It's not how you pick your nose;
it's where you put the boogers."

It has been observed many times that we live in a coarser,
cruder, angrier society than we did twenty—or even ten—
years ago. Ms. Manners may be a best-selling etiquette guru,
but from what I can see around me every day, very few
people follow her advice.

How do we reverse the rudeness trend? In Jack Ritchie's
short story "All the Rude People," when the main character
finds out he is terminally ill, he decides to combat rudeness

by executing all the rude people. The result? A "wave of politeness" sweeps the city, the evening news soon reports.

While you shouldn't shoot people for not saying, "Excuse me," consultant Ilise Benun suggests that we should confront rude behavior, not put up with it.

"When someone says something inappropriate to you, pause and then ask: 'Is there a reason for you saying that to me?'" suggests Benun.

I have started using this technique, and it works wonders. People are rude only when they think they can get away with it. When you "call them on the carpet" for their behavior, the behavior usually ceases and an apology is usually forthcoming. Try it and let me know.

GRACE

~

GRACE IS DOING FOR ANOTHER BEING KINDNESSES he doesn't deserve, hasn't earned, could not ask for, and can't repay. Its main facets are beauty, kindness, gratitude, charm, favor, and thankfulness. Grace offers man what he cannot do for himself. The unwritten creed of many is that God is under obligation to them, but grace suggests that we are under obligation to God. To live in that consciousness is to live by grace. Living by grace is costly; it means sharing. It has no meaning apart from a spirit of self-sacrifice that prompts the soul to think more of giving than of receiving, of caring for others rather than for one's self.

—PAUL S. MCELROY, *QUIET THOUGHTS*,
PETER PAUPER PRESS

Get a life in which you are generous. Look around at the azaleas making fuchsia starbursts in spring; look at a full moon hanging silver in a black sky on a cold night. And realize that life is glorious, and that you have no business taking it for granted. Care so deeply about its goodness that you want to spread it around. Take the money you would have spent on [entertainment] and give it to charity. Work in a soup kitchen. Tutor a seventh-grader. All of us want to do well. But if we do not do good, too, then doing well will never be enough.

—Anna Quindlen, *A Short Guide to a Happy Life*,

Do you live a life full of grace? Are you deeply thankful, on a daily basis, for all you have received?

To live in a state of grace, you must give generously to others in the spirit of love and service. But are you being generous enough? Here's a simple and automatic way to increase your generosity.

Most days, we probably make a dozen or more quick decisions that boil down to whether to be greedy or generous, to favor others or ourselves. For instance, a reader of one of my how-to books calls me for advice on how to start a business. Do I answer her question? Or tell her I'm too busy and to arrange a paid consultation for next month? Last night a man delivered takeout Chinese food to our door. Do I search for exact change for the tip, which should be around $2, or just let him keep the $3 change from the twenty- and five-dollar bills I gave him for a $22 order?

When in doubt, don't think about it; automatically opt for the more generous option. Answer the question. Give the extra dollar. Not only will you help others and feel good, but you'll avoid agonizing over simple things. It's truly a win-win situation.

HEALTH

~

WE TAKE OUR HEALTH FOR GRANTED. UNTIL WE GET sick. This I know from firsthand experience.

When I tell people I had a stroke, they're shocked. "At your age?" they ask incredulously, making me feel both feeble and guilty at the same time.

In my mind, I sort of agree with their quick assessment of me as someone less than virile. After all, guys my age (I'm forty-four) aren't supposed to get strokes.

Or are we? According to the National Stroke Council, strokes kill 150,000 Americans each year and leave another 200,000 disabled. And one out of three of these stroke victims is under sixty-five. Someone has a stroke in this country every fifty-three seconds.

Many stroke-related deaths and disabilities could be prevented if the public was better educated about stroke and its warning signs, prevention, and treatment. I wasn't, and my ignorance and stupidity nearly cost me my life.

Here's how it happened.

A few months ago, while I was on the telephone with a client, I became temporarily unable to speak or take notes with a pen. When these symptoms disappeared after about thirty seconds, I did the second stupidest thing I ever did in my life: I ignored them and went back to work.

What I had suffered, my family doctor, Phil Desplat, told me about a month later, was a TIA, or Transient Ischemic Attack.

Dr. Desplat explained that a TIA, which is a temporary decrease of blood flow to the brain, is a warning sign of an impending stroke. In fact, a stroke is simply an interruption of the blood supply to the brain.

Like many men my age, I foolishly prided myself on the fact that I never got sick and never went to the doctor. I went on with my work, which included a weeklong business trip to Bonn and Warsaw, where I ate large cholesterol-laden German and Polish dinners every night.

The day after I returned, about four weeks after my first episode, I again experienced loss of speech, although less severe. I also felt dizzy and off center, starting at around 11 P.M. Since it was late, and I was tired, I did the stupidest thing I ever did in my life: I hoped it would go away with a good night's sleep, and I went to bed.

In the morning, when I was still dizzy and off center, I began to worry and drove to Dr. Desplat's office. After a brief examination, he told me I was probably having a stroke and should go immediately to the emergency room. "And don't drive; have your wife drive you," he said, sternly adding, "You shouldn't have driven yourself here."

I was in the hospital a full week because the doctors had trouble finding the right combination of drugs to control my blood pressure, which got as high as 194 over 110.

After a few days, a combination of Atenolol and Zestoretic

brought my blood pressure down to an acceptable 120 over 80, and I was allowed to return home. Zestoretic contains a diuretic, so I, with a once-iron bladder, now urinated as frequently as a seventy-five year-old with prostate problems. The condition has since subsided.

Tests in the hospital and afterward showed that I had lost about 30 percent of my strength, balance, and coordination, mostly on my right side. During the first few days in the hospital, I couldn't brush my teeth or shave. And when I walked, my right leg dragged behind me.

Dr. Desplat later explained to me that the blood loss to my brain was caused by *thrombosis*: a clot had blocked a blood vessel going to the brain. Many other stroke patients suffer from *hemorrhage*, where a blood vessel in the brain ruptures, or *embolism*, where a lump of fat dislodges from the heart or arteries and gets stuck in the small blood vessels leading to the brain.

What could I do to prevent this from happening again? Dr. Alan Grossman, my cardiologist, gave me advice that was simple and expected: Eat less, lose weight, go on a low-fat and low-sodium diet, avoid caffeine, and exercise more. He also told me to take 400 micrograms a day of folic acid to lower my slightly elevated homocysteine level, a condition known to increase risk of cardiovascular illness.

I would need physical therapy to regain—as much as I could—the function stroke had taken away from me. Dr. Grossman also advised me to "slow down" at the office. But being a workaholic, I just couldn't do it.

The loss of strength and coordination didn't bother me as much as you might think. The reason: I lead a pretty sedentary life, and I don't need a lot of muscle to operate the TV remote control. But I signed on for the eight weeks of physical therapy my HMO was willing to pay for.

The exercise was a shock to my system, since prior to my stroke I didn't exercise. I liked the treadmill and bought one for our home; I could never get the hang of the Stairmaster and stopped it when therapy was over.

To help me regain my balance, my physical therapist had me stand on a small trampoline on one foot while he tossed a ball—usually low or to the side—for me to catch. He also had me walk backwards and sideways a lot. All of this was difficult, and when I left therapy after my eight weeks of managed care were up, I dropped it.

The loss of coordination in my right hand worried me considerably more, since as a freelance writer who gets paid according to his output, I need to be able to operate a PC keyboard at high speed.

I realized I could always buy voice-recognition software, but it held no appeal for me. Keyboarding is one of the few physical activities I actually enjoy doing.

The first time I tried to write, I was visibly slowed; the ring finger and pinkie of my right hand kept banging into the wrong keys. But within a few days, this difficulty vanished. Within a week, I was up to my full ninety-plus words a minute.

I am a living example of a simple stroke truth: The part of

your body you exercise most and soonest after your stroke is the part that recuperates the best and the fastest. In my case, it was the coordination in my right hand, which has now returned 100 percent. Conversely, the less you do and the longer you wait, the less strength and coordination you'll regain in that area.

I didn't stick with the balance exercises because, masked by my couch-potato lifestyle, I didn't seem to need it. I was okay walking up the stairs or across the street.

But a Cub Scout hike with my eight-year-old son's troop dramatized how not okay I really was. I stumbled constantly and fell several times on the rough, rocky trail. And I could not maintain my balance on a log crossing a stream; I slipped, muddied my pant leg, and soaked my sneaker in the cold, swiftly running water.

The wet foot didn't bother me, but the embarrassment did. For the first time, I felt like an old man—a "stroke victim." But laziness and the typical busy schedule of modern life have prevented me from returning to the physical therapist so far.

And my balance in hiking situations is still a source of difficulty and embarrassment. On a more recent family hike, the rugged naturalist leading the group seemed puzzled that I was hesitant to cross a stream over slippery stones.

"He had a stroke," my wife told him loudly enough for everyone in the group to hear, turn their heads, and stare in amazement. I suppose more of these awkward moments await me.

If I could wave a magic wand and make one change in the world with regard to stroke, it would be to make sure every adult—no matter what age—knows the early warning signs of stroke and what to do about them.

The "what to do" part is simple. Call your doctor and have someone drive you straight to the emergency room. If you're having a TIA, the doctors can take steps to bring your blood pressure down, and by following their advice and treatment, you can avoid a full-blown stroke.

If you're having a stroke, a trip to the ER can get it under control and minimize or eliminate any serious long-term damage. For example, if given within three hours after the stroke starts, a new drug, TPA (tissue plasminogen activator), can actually reverse paralysis and cause vision to return.

I've already described two early warning signs of stroke that rendered me temporarily unable to speak or use a pen.

The first is *weakness or numbness in an arm or leg,* or loss of use of that limb. The second is *slurred speech* ranging from difficulty in pronouncing words to a total inability to talk.

Other early warning signs of stroke include:

- Temporary vision problems—blurring, dimming, or blindness in one eye.

- A temporary inability to understand what others are saying or to make sense of words while reading.

- Tingling or numbness around the mouth, usually restricted to one side.

- Dizziness or the feeling of being "off center," which I also had.

Without being overly dramatic, let me give you a piece of advice I beg you to follow—even if it seems hokey to you now. Photocopy this page. Highlight the warning signs with a yellow marker and tape the page to your refrigerator door.

Dramatic, I know. Unnecessary for you? I hope. But do it anyway. Why?

I once took my health for granted . . . until God sent me a lesson that said I should pay more attention. I don't want you to have to get a lesson from God before you start paying more attention to your health. So please post the list as I suggest. It just might save your life.

Hired Help
(Outsourcing)

~

Decades ago, Joe Karbo, a mail-order entrepreneur, got rich running a full-page ad with the headline "The Lazy Man's Way to Riches."

What struck me was the subheadline: "Most people are too busy earning a living to make any money." Like most people today, I'm too busy making money—earning a living—to do anything else. But I have found a solution that works: outsourcing.

Outsourcing means hiring someone else to do a task for you. I'm grateful that we live in a society in which outsourcing, once a rarity, has become the norm.

In the pioneer days, people did everything themselves. If they wanted bread and butter, they baked the bread and churned the butter. If they wanted a cotton shirt, they planted the cotton and spun the thread.

In today's busy, specialized society, we don't have time to churn butter or sew our own clothes, so we hire other people to do these things (or buy the products ready-made).

Like a corporation (which, with my accountant's help, I've actually become), I outsource tasks that are outside what the management consultants call "my areas of core competence." And since there isn't much at which I'm competent, this includes nearly everything. For instance, I didn't complete the forms required to form the Limited Liability Corporation I own today; I paid my accountant to do it.

Amy, my wife, hates my outsourcing. "Why can't you be more like my father?" she asks.

Amy spent her childhood watching her father, Tom, constantly putter around the house, going from project to project with toolbox in hand. He was so good at it, in fact, that he made a handsome second income buying old houses, repairing them, and selling them.

I have no such skill, and in fact I shun manual labor in a most unmanly way.

Part of this I attribute to early failures. When we moved from a city apartment to our first home in the suburbs, I started with something small: mounting a tie rack on my closet door. Within two seconds I had drilled through the door instead of merely into it, leaving two gaping holes I had no idea how to plug. The drill promptly went into the pantry drawer, and I haven't touched it since.

Two other of my finest attributes—cowardliness and laziness—make the Yellow Pages and its inviting listings of local service firms my constant companion.

That first night in our new home, we went to a house party welcoming us onto the block. When we got home, the basement floor was littered with feces and toilet paper, though we had neither pets nor children at the time.

I was convinced our new suburbanite neighbors hated us

because we were city slickers, and were trying to terrorize us into leaving. Ben, a kindly next-door neighbor, suggested we call Roto-Rooter. Turns out a tree root had picked that night to completely block the line running from the house to the sewer, causing the sewage to back up into the lowest point in our plumbing system—a shower in the basement.

That trauma convinced me I could never master the complexities of home repair—but folks like Roto Rooter could. Why learn how to use a plumber's snake when I could let my fingers do the walking? The job got done right, and I avoided time, effort, and frustration—a win-win deal.

The idea of picking up a phone instead of a screwdriver appealed to my lazy side (which today, according to Amy, is the only one I have left). As the years passed, I've gradually outsourced more and more, and done less and less.

Lawn Alive fertilizes and mows my lawn. Toth Plumbing fixes the toilet when it runs. PCM Data Processing keeps my books, and Wayne Kolb prepares my tax returns. Annette vacuums my office and my home.

I'm fast approaching the perfect life, where all I do is sit at my computer and type all day long, then go home, eat, play with the kids, and read or watch TV. (I don't even do anything but write on the computer; George, my "computer guy," loads software and installs system upgrades, like DSL, when their times have come. I even pay him to teach me how to use these programs and tools—I don't have the time to read the manuals.)

Do I feel guilty about any of this appalling self-indulgence? Somewhat. But here's my philosophy: Your most precious resource is time, and it is nonrenewable. You can't get it back again. Money, on the other hand . . . well, you can *always* make more. My path has been to buy time with money, then make more money with some of the time I've purchased.

Following my "Lazy Man's Way," have I gotten rich, like Joe Karbo promised? I think so. By turning my energies toward my work, which I love, instead of the minutiae of life, which I detest, I've actually increased my earnings—and through hard work and investing, we've reached a point of comfort, if not opulence. In my opinion, my outsourcing has definitely paid off and returned the investment I've spent on services many times over.

But more important, outsourcing has given me my life— or at least, the life I've wanted and enjoyed—including time with Amy, time with my sons Alex and Stephen, time for me, time to write and think and read, and a career I love. Now, if only I can find something to really impress my wife—like replacing the toilet seat.

Thank God I'm not a pioneer!

Hot Dogs

~

In a recent Sally Forth cartoon showing Sally relaxing in a bubble bath, Sally observed, "Baths are to showers as filet mignon is to hot dogs."

I'd reverse the statement, because I'm one of those people who prefer hot dogs to filet mignon.

The ranks of hot-dog lovers are legion, and we consider biting into a red-hot wiener one of the sublime pleasures of life. Food can be a great comfort in times of stress and need, and hot dogs are one of those inexpensive pleasures that warm me from the inside out.

Filet mignon, caviar, fine port, and pheasant are pleasures reserved for the rich, but anyone can enjoy a foot-long with mustard and relish.

Still only about a buck today, hot dogs are one of the tastiest and most affordable meals.

Hot dogs—also known as franks, frankfurters, or wieners—were ranked as America's third-favorite food in 1994 behind pizza (#1) and sandwiches (#2). If you were to place all the hot dogs consumed in the United States each year end to end, they'd reach to the moon and back three times.

Every year, Americans eat about twenty billion hot dogs. Between Memorial Day and Labor Day alone this year, Americans will eat five billion hot dogs, reports Oscar

Mayer. If these hot dogs were laid end to end, they would form a link of dogs five-hundred times longer than the distance between California and New York.

According to the National Hot Dog and Sausage Council, 95 percent of Americans serve hot dogs in their homes. The average American eats eighty hot dogs a year.

Hot dogs are a staple of American culinary culture from backyard barbecues to ball games. Like Dr. Seuss's green eggs and ham, people will eat hot dogs anywhere—and they can, since hot dogs are a uniquely portable food: meat in a tube with a casing and roll to prevent spillage, mess, and burned hands. "It has been said that the most loyal and most noble dog of all is the hot dog," comments Burt Wolf, a New York food writer and restaurateur. "It feeds the hand that bites it."

While hot dogs are not health food, they are in fact healthier and less fattening than many other popular foods. A hot dog on a bun has only 260 calories, compared with 370 calories in a peanut-butter-and-jelly sandwich and 440 calories in a cheeseburger. That same hot dog contains 15 grams of fat, compared with 26 grams for a breaded fish sandwich on a roll with tartar sauce (the new low-fat hot dogs have 1 to 2 grams of fat each). Hot dogs were included on the NASA-approved menus for the Skylab and Apollo space missions.

The modern hot dog, a descendant of the sausages first concocted by the ancient Greeks, may have been invented in the 1850s by an enterprising Austrian. He named his sausage "Wien" after Vienna, Austria.

There is another school of thought that maintains that the hot dog was invented by an ambitious butcher in Frankfurt on Main in Germany at about the same time. He called his tasty sausages "frankfurters."

Nathan Handwerker, founder of Nathan's Famous, is generally credited for making hot dogs popular in America. In 1916, with $300 he had saved, Nathan opened his first stand at the corner of Surf and Stillwell Avenues in Coney Island, New York, where he started selling hot dogs for five cents, a price that included a root beer and a pickle.

To promote sales of his hot dogs, Handwerker hired wholesome-looking young men to hang around his hot-dog carts and eat hot dogs in full view of people strolling the boardwalk. He dressed the young men in starched white coats to give the impression that they were doctors or interns (legend has it that he even had them carry stethoscopes in their pockets). Visitors to Coney Island figured that if the hot dogs, which only cost a nickel at the time, were being eaten by doctors, they had to be healthy.

IMAGINATION

~

THIS POWER OF IMAGINATION, THE MAKING OF some familiar object, as fire or rain, or a bucket or shovel, do new duty as an exponent of some truth or general law, bewitches and delights men. It is a taking of dead stocks, and clothing about with immortality; it is music out of creaking and scouring. All opaque things are transparent, and the light of heaven struggles through.

—RALPH WALDO EMERSON

One of the greatest powers possessed by humankind is imagination, the ability to dream and visualize things that do not exist except in the mind.

The Land of Oz. Superman. Tarzan. *Star Trek*. *Great Expectations*. Sherlock Holmes. Frankenstein's monster. *Paradise Lost*. Rubik's Cube. Holograms. Lasers. *20,000 Leagues Under the Sea*. *Journey to the Center of the Earth*. Ice cream. This is an infinitesimally small, partial listing of all the things imagination has given us.

Imagination seems to be nurtured by solitude, quiet, reading, and the ability to sit for long periods and do nothing but think—activities and environments considered unfashionable in today's productivity-obsessed, time-strapped world.

Do we risk busying ourselves out of imagination? I think so. The solution? Solitude and quiet time.

Make the time to daydream. Work it into your schedule. In practical terms, I recommend you schedule at least one hour a week for yourself during which you do nothing but sit and contemplate (or walk in the woods, if you prefer to be less sedentary).

The benefits? Improved mental health, greater serenity, stress reduction, peace, contentment, and as a bonus, more ideas. (The idea for this book, for instance, came during my weekly solitude hour.)

INDOOR PLUMBING

~

I LIKE VISITING HISTORICAL HOUSES. NOT JUST FOR the history lesson or to admire the crafts our forefathers produced. But to remind me how grateful I am that I live now instead of then.

Visit any historical house (and there are several in my county that date back to the Civil and Revolutionary Wars) and you can't help but notice what these homes don't have: toilets, running water, electric lights, electricity, heating.

Perhaps life was slower, less stressed, and less pressured then, but I don't think that's entirely true. Imagine in the winter having to go outside every time you had to go to the bathroom, or not being able to take a shower. The outhouses smelled, and so did the people.

Famed psychologist Abraham Maslow established a hierarchy of human needs, and the basics—which we take for granted now—were in extremely rudimentary stages a few hundred years ago. Don't you turn up the lights when it gets dark early in the winter? Before electric lights, people slept ten to eleven hours a day—instead of the current six to eight—simply because it was too dark to do much of anything else. What a waste!

Of all the basics, indoor plumbing has to rank at the top of the list. When people had to fill up an entire bathtub with one kettle of water at a time, baths were few and far between; one can only imagine how grimy folks felt. So when you take a hot shower tonight and brush your teeth in a comfortable modern bathroom, thank your lucky stars. Modern life has drawbacks but also advantages. And indoor plumbing is one of the latter.

JOKES

~

IN HER BOOK *365 WAYS TO GIVE THANKS*, BRENDA Shoshanna gives this advice: "Learn a few jokes and tell them."

It's very easy to brighten up a dull conversation or distract someone who's been complaining too long. Learn a few jokes and find a way to slip them into the conversation.

You can find many collections of jokes at a library or bookstore. Spend an hour copying the jokes that suit you. Then go home and memorize them. The next time you are stuck in a conversation that's going downhill, find a way to slip in one of your jokes. You'll be amazed at how quickly the mood changes. After you've done this a few times, return to the book and learn a few more jokes.

It's fun to tell someone else's joke, especially if you know how to deliver a joke, but my secret, small hobby is writing my own. They have given me pleasure over the years, and amused many adults and children.

Until now, these jokes have never been published in any book to my knowledge. Now I share them freely—my gift to you. Enjoy!

Q: Who is the smartest sister in the convent?
A: Nun the wiser.

Q: What do you call an Arab prince who owns a dairy?
A: A milk sheik.

Q: Where does Mickey Mouse's girlfriend shop?
A: In a Minnie Mall.

Q: What is the octopus's favorite game?
A: Eight ball.

Q: Where do optometrists dance?
A: At the eyeball.

Q: What animal asks a question?
A: An owl. ("Who?")

Q: Why do some psychologists use acupuncture in therapy sessions with patients?
A: To deflate their patients' egos.

Q: What thing says its name as it moves?
A: A choo-choo.

Q: Did you hear about the bees that were allergic to honey?
A: They broke out in hives.

Q: What do you call two physicians who go into practice together?
A: A pair-a-docs.

Q: What do teenage giraffes do on a date?
A: Neck.

Q: Where do kittens learn to wash themselves?
A: Cat-lick school.

Q: Why was the fortune-teller smiling?
A: She was a happy medium.

Q: Where do automobiles swim?
A: In a car pool.

Q: Where do cars eat their dinners?
A: On a license plate.

Q: What kind of music did the ghost orchestra play?
A: Spirituals and soul music.

Q: Why were prehistoric waitresses very polite?
A: They didn't want to make their diners sore.

Q: What snack do mermaids serve their kids?
A: Peanut butter and jellyfish.

Q: Where do spiders receive their e-mail?
A: At their web sites.

Q: Where does Batman brush his teeth?
A: In the bat-room.

Q: What happened to the short-tempered doctor?
A: He lost all his patients.

Q: Why did the FBI investigate the city aquarium?
A: They heard something fishy was going on there.

Q: Why did the skeleton get an F on his monster test?
A: He was a bonehead.

Q: What instrument does a Greek percussionist play?
A: An isosceles triangle.

JUNK FOOD

~

I CONFESS: I LOVE CHEEZ DOODLES. BUT AS I MUNCH them with guilty pleasure, I am forced to wonder how much they contribute to my daily nutritional requirements.

What food group, for instance, do Cheez Doodles belong to? According to the American Nutritional Society, there are four basic food groups: meat, bread and cereals, dairy, and fruits and vegetables.

Come to think of it, why do we bother grouping foods in the first place? I suppose it's human nature to force everything into its own little slot.

I think a lot of people have their own food groups. My wife's are probably pie, cake, ice cream, and cookies (amazingly, I'm overweight and she is not).

For my sons, Alex, 11, and Stephen, 8, it's pizza, McDonald's, Burger King, and a fourth category. Stephen's fourth category is probably spicy hot buffalo wings, while Alex favors exotic seafood including octopus and lobster.

Cheez Doodles belong to another food group, a favorite of junk-food lovers everywhere: the orange food group. In addition to Doodles, the main delicacies in this group are American cheese, Tang, orange soda, and Kraft Macaroni & Cheese.

The first thing that strikes me when I look at the label of the bag of Cheez Doodles on my desk is the massive amounts of ingredients other than cheese. Yes, there's a sprinkle of cheddar in there. But it's buried in a mixture of sodium caseinate, cottonseed oil, partially hydrogenated soybean oil (why not hydrogenate it all the way?), and modified cornstarch (how exactly do they change the starch—and to what?). Yum!

I'm reminded of comedian Sean Morey's complaint about Corn Pops cereal. "When I was a kid, they were Sugar Pops. Now they're Corn Pops. Who're they kidding? There's more corn in cigarettes."

Cheez Doodles, like Chinese food, also contain a healthy dose of monosodium glutamate. When a waiter in a Chinese restaurant asks, "Do you want MSG?" I answer, "I'll take it on the side." To me it's an odd question to ask; if MSG is optional, why include it in the first place?

Tip: If it is raining or even if the air is just humid, you can enhance the Cheez Doodle eating experience by leaving the bag open for a day. When the Doodles absorb ambient moisture, they soften for a nice, slow chew, and the excess moisture actually increases the intensity of the artificial cheese flavor.

I view Kraft macaroni and cheese as a Cheez Doodle-based pasta dish: elbow macaroni in a creamy sauce of Cheez Doodle powder, butter, and milk. A poor man's fettuccini alfredo.

Perhaps the most famous member of the orange food group is Tang orange-flavored drink. Now, if oranges already contain orange-flavored juice, why make a chemical powder of the same flavor that doesn't taste half as good?

In the 1960s, NASA discovered that orange juice was difficult to drink in outer space. Freeze-dried orange juice is difficult to rehydrate. Orange drink crystals mixed into water in space just made hard orange lumps. General Foods developed Tang, a synthetic powder that, when mixed with water, could be used by the astronauts in place of OJ.

Tang, along with other members of the orange food group, has gained a reputation as a repast of the lower class. On the sitcom *Married . . . with Children,* when Peg didn't cook Al a steak, he made his own dinner: dry Tang powder on white bread.

In keeping with orange as an out-of-vogue food color, cheese lovers consider American cheese a dairy product of the lower classes. But this scorn is from folks who scarf down blue cheese, which is basically curdled milk with mold growing all over it. So how much can they really know about what's good versus what's not?

Does an orange, natural and healthy, qualify as a member of the orange food group? Ironically, no. The natural skin of oranges is yellow-green; they are artificially dyed orange on the outside to increase their visual appeal to consumers. Why not just rename them "yellow-greens" and be done with it?

I know of no nutritionists who recommend any of the orange food group in their diets. But I refuse to let them discourage me. After all, if the orange food group is good enough for NASA, the folks who put a man on the moon, it's good enough for me.

Junk Mail

~

This short essay is in defense of my own profession: I am a direct mail writer.

There, I said it. And I'm proud of it.

The critics call direct mail "junk mail." But if you do that, you should call commercials "junk TV" and ads "junk newspaper pages."

As a direct mail professional, I know many people hate getting my mailings. They communicate their feeling by ripping up my sales letter, stuffing it in my reply envelope, and mailing the ripped up letter (instead of an order form and check) back to me in the reply envelope, which I have to pay the post office for.

But don't hate direct mail. We do a good service for you in many ways.

Professional speaker Dottie Walters has said, "Direct mail is the bazaar of the mind." Where else do you get so many ideas for free? Direct mail informs you of candidates' positions, invites you to theater and gallery openings, and offers you gourmet foods and coffees you can try in your home for a month for free.

How did this business of direct marketing start? In his book *I Wish I'd Thought of That!* Jeff Rovin reports:

By 1872, Aaron Montgomery Ward, a dry goods salesman, was tired of taking his goods from door-to-door. Selling mostly to farmers, he knew what rural America wanted and felt he had a better way of getting it to them. With $2,400, Ward and his brother-in-law stocked a 12-by-14 room in Chicago, printed a single sheet describing their merchandise, and sent it to all the customers on Ward's route.

Orders poured in and within two years, the one-page list had grown to a 72-page illustrated catalog. By 1884, there were 10,000 products in the 240-page Montgomery Ward Catalog and by the end of the century, sales had surpassed the $4 million mark.

But Ward's mailings were still aimed at rural America, and his catalog didn't encourage people to try new products: If you saw what you wanted, you ordered it. On the other hand, railroad clerk Richard Sears and watchmaker Alvah Roebuck wrote gloriously enticing copy for the goods in their Wondrous Emporium catalog, first published in 1886. They also had something for everyone, from iceboxes to wigs (they matched your color if you sent a sample of hair) to "bust food," which (so they said) increased the size of a lady's bosom.

According to the Direct Marketing Association, an industry trade group, the catalog market—estimated at $78.3 billion in 1997—is expected to reach $106.8 billion by 2002. That's a compound growth rate of 6.3 percent. In 1997, 257,900 Americans were employed in the catalog industry, which mailed more than thirteen billion catalogs. By 2002, catalog marketers will employ 485,400 people.

Lester Wunderman, an ad agency executive, invented the term *direct marketing* in the 1960s. He has probably created more successful mail-order ads and direct mail packages than anyone in the country. His creations include the Columbia House Record Club, American Express, L.L. Bean, and Gevalia Kaffe, the first mail-order coffee.

But Wunderman sees the future of direct marketing based in electronics, not paper. In his autobiography, *On Being Direct*, Wunderman writes:

> Video on demand, home shopping, on-line games, and directory services will become increasingly convenient and less costly. We can see the beginning of a revolutionary new communication, information, and entertainment shopping system. The information superhighway will likely be some combination of telephone, broadcast and cable TV, and local area computer networks. It is not clear who will pay for what, but the consumer will be empowered as never before. Video on demand, advertising on demand, and shopping on demand will change the way consumers shop.

Most important, nonprofits use direct mail to do good works. They raise money to feed starving people, cure diseases, save endangered species, and grant the fondest wishes of terminally ill children. What's "junky" about that?

LAUGHTER

~

I REMEMBERED HAVING READ, TEN YEARS OR SO earlier, Hans Selye's classic book, *The Stress of Life*. With great clarity, Selye showed that adrenal exhaustion could be caused by emotional tension, such as frustration or suppressed rage. He detailed the negative effects of the negative emotions on body chemistry.

The inevitable question arose in my mind: what about the positive emotions? If negative emotions produce negative chemical changes in the body, wouldn't the positive emotions produce positive chemical changes? Is it possible that love, faith, laughter, confidence, and the will to live have therapeutic value?

How scientific was it to believe that laughter—as well as the positive emotions in general—was affecting my body chemistry for the better? If laughter did in fact have a salutary effect on the body's chemistry, it seemed at least theoretically likely that it would enhance the system's ability to fight the inflammation. So we took sedimentation rate readings just before as well as several hours after the laughter episodes. Each time, there was a drop of at least five points. The drop by itself was not substantial, but it held and was cumulative. I was greatly elated by the discovery that there is a physiologic basis for the ancient theory that laughter is good medicine.

—NORMAN COUSINS, *ANATOMY OF AN ILLNESS*,

BANTAM BOOKS

There is something strange about me only a few friends and relatives know (most people never notice): I don't laugh. Never? Well, hardly ever. You can count the number of times I laugh in a year on one hand and still have several fingers left over.

Am I humorless? Far from it. It's just an odd psychological/physiological trait. Humor amuses me. And when it does, I smile. That's how I laugh. But as far as laughing out loud, whatever switch sets that off inside most people is missing from me.

I've compensated over the years by making others laugh. In elementary school, I was the class clown. In social situations, I wisecrack and joke. It brings me pleasure, and I've been told by those around me it does the same for them. I share the pleasure. But not the laughs. I just can't.

Do you laugh? If you do, count it as a blessing. You have something I don't, and wish I did. Use it often. Maybe it will catch on and I'll laugh too.

LOVE

~

LOVE NEVER FAILS: BUT WHETHER THERE ARE
prophecies, they will fail; whether there be tongues, they
will cease; whether there be knowledge, it will vanish
away. For we know in part, and we prophesy in part. But
when that which is perfect has come, then that which is
in part will be done away. When I was a child, I spoke as
a child, I understood as a child, I thought as a child; but
when I became a man, I put away childish things. For
now we see in a mirror, darkly, but then face to face. Now
I know in part; but then I shall know just as also I am
known. And now abideth faith, hope, love, these three;
but the greatest of these is love.

—1 COR. 13:8–13

Everyone has asked himself the great question of antiq-
uity as of the modern world: What is the *summum bonum*—
the supreme good? You have life before you. Once only
you can live it. What is the noblest object of desire, the
supreme gift to covet?

We have been accustomed to be told that the greatest
thing in the religious world is *faith*. That great word has
been the keynote for centuries of the popular religion; and
we have easily learned to look upon it as the greatest thing

in the world. Well, we are wrong. If we have been told that, we may miss the mark. I have taken you in the chapter which I have just read, to Christianity at its source, and there we have seen, "The greatest of these is love." It is not an oversight. Paul was speaking of faith just a moment before. He says, "If I have all Faith, so that I can remove mountains, and have not Love; I am nothing." So far from forgetting he deliberately contrasts them, "Now abideth Faith, Hope, Love," and without a moment's hesitation the decision falls, "The greatest of these is Love."

—HENRY DRUMMOND, *THE GREATEST THING IN THE WORLD*, PETER PAUPER PRESS

In love, I have no special expertise. I'm pretty typical in this area: I have a wife and two children, a sister, and a mother, and my love for them is profound and powerful.

The one thing I can tell you is that, if you don't have love in your life, you're missing a lot. I have lots of unattached and single friends, and lots of friends without family or children; and it seems to me they avoid these attachments out of fear. Fear of commitment, fear of risking rejection or hurt, fear of responsibility, fear of losing control.

To these folks I say: Come out of your shell and take the risk! Yes, you can get hurt in love. But without love you're living only half a life. And the paradox is this: You can't appreciate what you're missing until you have it. And it's a reward worth pursuing.

LOVED ONES WHO HAVE PASSED AWAY

~

IT'S ALL VERY SAD HOW WE LOVE PEOPLE AND THEY are so fiercely individual and so priceless and they pass away and then as we in turn pass away into oblivion their memories are gone. It's the eternal drama of a species, of time burying the dead. The wheels keep turning.

—JOYCE CAROL OATES, CITED IN *ENDANGERED SPECIES* BY LAWRENCE GROBEL, DE CAPO PRESS

By all means, grieve for life lost. But celebrate the life that person lived.

It's ironic. Death is inevitable. Everyone dies. Yet, when a loved one dies, the loss—even though expected—is nearly unbearable. Why is that so?

When my father passed away after a long struggle with cancer, I became enraged at God. At seventy, Dad was a relatively young man. After he worked so hard to lift himself from poverty and raise a family, how unfair that he be cut off from the last and possibly most pleasurable portion of his life! Unfairly, I began to resent the people I knew who were in their mid to late eighties with no ill health. Why couldn't Dad have had as much time as they were enjoying?

But to look at it from the opposite point of view: Dad lived a full life. At seventy, he had experienced the joys of a successful career, a home, loving wife, loving children, good friends, and adoring grandchildren. Most of what people hope to experience during a lifetime he had in fact done. When I gave the eulogy at his funeral, I began by saying, "Everybody wants to be happy. And my father knew the secret of happiness." It was, of course, living for others—whether doing a kind deed for a neighbor, making my mother and us kids happy, or teaching children he met at a lake or pond to fish.

While I felt robbed of the five or ten additional years I might have had with him, I'm grateful for the seventy wonderful years we did have. While it broke my heart that my youngest son, who was three when my father died, probably won't have clear memories of him, at least he was born—and they were together for several years—before Dad passed away.

Everything ends. If the thing is good, we mourn its passing. But at least, for a time, we had the good thing. That's a powerful life reward. Said William Buchanan, "The general outlook is not that the person has died but that the person has lived."

In her book *365 Ways to Give Thanks,* Brenda Shoshanna gives the following sensible advice for coping with the death of a loved one:

> The best way to recover and heal from loss is to truly integrate all of the goodness and lessons the life of the person

you lost brought to you. We all want a sense of continuity. We want to know that who that person was and what they gave is not lost forever.

Take some time to think carefully about the life of the person who has passed away and how they can be best honored for the way they lived. What was most important to them? What work did they leave unfinished? What mistakes did they make that you might like to see corrected?

Take some appropriate action on your loved one's behalf and dedicate it to him or her. The best memorial for another person is a life well lived, evidence that the person's positive influence continues.

MARRIAGE

~

HAVE YOU NOT SEEN FROM SOME VANTAGE POINT the confluence of two great rivers? And have you remarked how one, like the rapid flowing Blue Nile, carries with it even to the delta far away much of the rich muddy soil from the country through which it passes? Beside it moves the slower river from the plains, the White Nile, clear by comparison. Once joined together these two great rivers are distinguishable for miles as they flow side by side in the same riverbed. They are separate yet united. So, too, when two separate yet loving hearts begin to live their lives together they may for some time go side by side, like two merged streams not fully united, yet the longer they stay together the more they have in common, continually losing some of their identity until they become as one. Each becomes an inseparable part of the other—as they become a family. Two people, husband and wife, may, like a river, later separate but the whole is diminished thereby and part of one goes with part of the other.

—PAUL S. MCELROY, *QUIET THOUGHTS*,
PETER PAUPER PRESS

Marriage is the biggest mixed bag I know. It can go from bliss to battlefield over something as inconsequential as a set of lost keys or who forgot to walk the dog or whose turn it is to take out the garbage.

But think about it: When all is said and done, you love your spouse, right? That makes it all worthwhile.

My wife, raging with anger at something wrong I'd done, said, "I don't like you right now—but I always love you." If you can take that position, you can get through the tough stuff and enjoy the good.

Ben Franklin, when evaluating anything, always made a list of pros and cons. Yes, a good marriage can be work, but look at all the pros. You get the intense love and affection of another human being who accepts you for who and what you are. You have constant companionship that protects you against loneliness and isolation. You get a family, which is a meaningful part of any human being's life.

I think Ben Franklin would have approved.

Material Possessions

(And enjoying them for what they are, but recognizing
their place in the grander scheme of life)

~

THE TEN COMMANDMENTS TELL US NOT TO COVET things, but most of us spend our lives pining for useless things we don't need: designer clothes, a bigger house, and a fancier car. My attitude is, if you have a roof over your head and food to eat, be thankful. You really don't need anything else.

Personally, I've never been into status or status symbols; I drove a 1984 two-door Chevette well into my thirties. My disinterest in luxury items probably stems from my father. Driving around Paterson, New Jersey, where he had his insurance office, he often pointed out the new luxury cars parked in front of run-down tenements and said, "These people have no money, but they all have Cadillacs." The message was clear: People who bought stuff they couldn't really afford were ignorant and deserved pity.

I have no desire to drive a BMW or Lexus. When friends ooh and ah over fine crystal or silver they have bought, I silently disapprove. Who needs more stuff to fuss over?

The sole exception in my life to this rule (nobody's perfect) was Monty, my beloved Montblanc pen. I didn't have to pay for him; he was a gift from Sprint to me for using their long-distance service.

I had heard of Montblanc and knew it was considered a fine pen, but the thought of paying over a hundred dollars for one when I could get a perfectly good Bic for ninety-nine cents at CVS had always struck me as the worst sort of self-indulgence. But for free, owning the pen seemed somehow acceptable; and besides, I needed a pen. I called Sprint and gave them Monty's order code.

When Monty arrived, it was love at first sight. Worth a hundred bucks? I have no idea. But for free, I loved how my thick-bodied pen fit my grip so well. And the exceptionally smooth writing of its ballpoint was—for a writer—sheer delight.

I soon noticed that Montblanc owners were a "secret society," with members from all walks of life. The wealthy CEO of one of my clients had a Montblanc. But I also noticed one in the hands of a toner-stained repairman who came to my office to fix my copier.

That's the nice thing about luxury items in the lower price categories: Everyone can really afford one, if he or she wants the thing badly enough. Not many people can pay cash for a brand new Lexus; but almost everyone can cough up enough for a shiny new Montblanc, if they ferret away paychecks for a week or two.

Owning Monty gave me the same regal feeling I imagine a five thousand square-foot home in an upper-crust neighborhood might bestow. I was a man of distinction (or, more accurately, a man with a distinct pen).

But with great possessions comes great responsibility, which I didn't like.

Before Monty, I lost pens all the time. Nothing to worry about—I'd just go to CVS, plunk down another dollar, and buy another Bic. But Monty, retailing at the price of a hundred Bics, would not be so cheap to replace.

I began to obsess about Monty, patting my shirt pocket about three times an hour to make sure he was still there. I even started referring to him by name, which amused my wife and children to no end. If I put Monty down and forgot to pick him up again, I would panic when I found he was missing—and rest only when he was safely back in his pocket again.

The inevitable finally happened: I lost Monty forever. I walked out of a Friendly's and realized Monty wasn't with me. But though I returned to the table less than a minute later, it was too late.

I could not understand why the restaurant manager did not consider Monty's loss—which I immediately hinted was probable theft on the part of the waitress, who knew value when she saw it—as tragic or important as I did. I worked up considerable anger, and extracted from him the promise of a phone call the minute Monty was found (translation: when the waitress, racked with guilt, confessed her crime and returned the stolen goods).

But the call never came, and as weeks passed, I gradually came to accept my loss.

With Monty's disappearance came an odd feeling of relief.

No longer did I pat my pocket three times an hour or make sure Monty was sticking out of the top of it so people would take notice. I was no longer part of the elite. And I liked the fact that I wasn't weighed down by the burden of material possessions and could go on with the rest of my life.

I learned that materialism never was and never will be for me. The less junk I have, the better.

While my luxury-free lifestyle may not be for everyone, I suspect that we all own too much stuff to comprehend, and the overload prevents us from fully appreciating what we have.

So the next time you have the urge to splurge, don't. Instead, put the money in the bank, keep it in your pocket, give it to charity, or buy a present for a child you love and watch his or her face light up in delight. The feeling of peace and contentment you get is the greatest luxury you can buy yourself—with or without Sprint bonus points.

Modern Medicine

~

Benjamin Franklin said that nothing in this world is certain but death and taxes. But there's a third item he left off his list: As you get older, you'll have to take a lot of pills.

As a child, I giggled when my grandfather went through his morning routine at the breakfast table. He took sixteen pills with his juice, naming each one and explaining its purpose ("This is for liver function") before popping it. He also liked his eggs so loose he could have skipped the juice and washed the pills down with undercooked egg white.

In my middle age, I'm no longer giggling. To control my blood pressure and cholesterol, I take 100 milligrams of Atenolol, 50 milligrams of Zestoretic, 45 milligrams of Pravachol, and to top it off, a coated 325-milligram Enteric aspirin.

Taking these pills is a burden. To make sure I don't forget any, I take them all at the same time, even though the prescriptions advise different times of days for different ones. On road trips, I have often had my doctor make an emergency call to an out-of-town pharmacy so I could get the stash I forgot to pack.

Back at home, the pills never run out at the same time, so at times CVS seems like my second home. And the doctor always decides to go on vacation just as I'm out of refills and need a new prescription called in.

Taking pills doesn't end for me with prescription medicines, either. I take a daily multivitamin because my tongue suffers from vitamin deficiency. Without a One-a-Day tablet, it becomes supersensitive, causing irritating pain and salivation whenever it rubs against my teeth—an event that is difficult to prevent inside your mouth.

Then there's vitamin C for preventing a sniffle or ache from blossoming into a full-blown cold or flu. I choke on the thousand-milligram tablets the size and shape of a small football. Cutting them in half releases a chalky powder that makes me gag even worse.

Now well-meaning friends are telling me to take even more pills. These people have good intentions, but their meddling can make statements about me that are less than flattering: If you tell me to try a fat burner, how can I possibly conclude that you don't think I'm a porker?

A colleague sent me a bottle of tablets labeled "Anti-Aging System: A Dietary Supplement for Men." I didn't take them because I think it's too late: I'm already aging.

In college I sometimes took caffeine pills to help me pull all-nighters. Now one cup of coffee does the trick, and I frequently have insomnia. I've tried sleeping pills. They put me in a relaxed state that, alas, doesn't involve sleep; instead I lie awake in the dark.

One's choice of pills sometimes makes a lifestyle statement. A company sent me a mailing offering its two products, one to increase male potency and one to promote a healthy prostate. The objectives overlap, and many of the ingredients—saw palmetto, nettle, yohimbe, avena sativa, ginseng, and ginkgo biloba—were the same. Did I want to have more sex or make fewer trips to the proctologist's office? Both seemed worthy goals.

Despite the cost of taking all these pills, more Americans are popping them than ever before, because they realize the blessings of modern medicine (better health, longer life) outweigh the minor inconveniences I've described.

As my health declines, my pill consumption will only multiply. I see myself, content in my old age, reciting the medications and their functions to my grandchildren at breakfast, as my grandfather did for me. Only I won't be able to do it with eggs, which I love, on account of my high cholesterol. I'll probably be eating oatmeal or bran flakes instead of two eggs sunny-side up, bacon, and buttered toast. But considering the payoff, that's really not such a bitter pill to swallow.

MONEY

~

MONEY IS LIKE MANURE. IF YOU SPREAD IT AROUND, it does a lot of good, but if you pile it up in one place, it stinks.

—CLINT W. MURCHISON

Remember that money is of a prolific, generating nature. Money can beget money, and its offspring can beget more, and so on. Five shillings turned is six; turned again it is seven; and so on till it becomes a hundred pounds. The more there is of it, the more it produces at every turning, so that the profits rise quicker and quicker. He that murders a crown destroys all that it might have produced.

—BENJAMIN FRANKLIN

When the Rivera United Methodist Church in Redondo Beach, California needed more money than the Sunday collections were bringing in, the Rev. Orlie White remembered the biblical parable of the talents. Putting that parable into practice, Rev. White filled a collection plate with $10 bills and invited each of his 200 parishioners to take one. He asked them to use the money to make more money, then return the original $10 and the amount it had earned to the church.

One woman brought needles and yarn out and crocheted covers for clothes hangers, which she sold for a profit of $38. Another used the money to enter a bowling tournament and won a $75 prize for the church. A man and his wife pooled their stake and bought a share of stock for $20; three months later, they sold it for more than $50.

By the end of the year, the original $2,000 had grown into $8,000.

—Arthur F. Lenehan, *The Best of Bits and Pieces*,
The Economics Press, Inc.

My father once told me, "Money is not important, as long as you're happy." But I disagree. Seminar leader Ted Nicholas says that money is one of the four elements of a happy life. I share Ted's view.

The blessing is not money per se, but what money can do for you. With enough money, you can feed and shelter your family, keep them healthy with good medical care, and have enough material possessions to ensure joy (both children and adults need their toys). You can also share your money or possessions with those who don't have as much.

Poverty makes life brutal. Acquire enough money to achieve comfort and security. It's what God wants you to do.

MUSIC

~

WHEN I WAS A TEENAGER, I WORKED ONE SUMMER IN the warehouse for a company that distributed electronic components. Most of the laborers outside of the office were unskilled. The notable exception was Wilson, an electronics technician responsible for testing components and other quality inspection procedures.

Wilson fascinated me because he was intelligent and had eclectic taste in many things, including art, clothes, and music. I was into jazz, and all day in his lab area he played jazz musicians whom I didn't know but thought I should. I liked what I heard, and started to tune my radio at home to his station. (The money from the job was for college tuition and could not be wasted on luxuries like records.)

One day while Wilson was in the back getting a tool, a warehouse worker, not realizing the radio was Wilson's, changed it to a country music station when he walked by. When Wilson came back, I saw that he noticed the change. I caught the other worker's eye, and gave him a knowing glance and a sour face to indicate, yes, the two of us cats, we're too sophisticated for this honky-tonk tune.

But instead of returning my sarcastic grin in camaraderie, Wilson shook his head and told me, "*All* music is good."

As a youngster who favored classical and jazz in the 1960s

during the Beatles' rock 'n' roll invasion of America, I took a defensive and snobbish attitude toward music I didn't like. But as I grew older, I realized Wilson is right: *All* music is good.

At work, I listen to music all day in the background as I write; I abhor complete silence. And while I don't concentrate on the music as I work, it has enough influence that I choose specific music to enhance or even modify my mood as it fits my work.

For instance, if I am doing some thinking that requires quiet contemplation, I may put on Beethoven's *Moonlight Sonata* or Bach's *Brandenburg Concerto*. When I am working at a steady pace, Top 40 rock on the radio keeps me going. If I find my energy waning, I boost it up with hard rock or hot jazz.

With the trend today toward excess violence, sex, and obscenity, especially in rap and hip-hop, Wilson's "all music is good" rule may no longer hold in every instance. But do I think these artists should be kept off radio or have their CDs destroyed? No. Because if you and I don't like what they're singing, we can simply change the station.

MUSTARD

~

SINCE HOT DOGS ARE MY FAVORITE FOOD, IT'S ONLY natural that mustard is my favorite condiment. I use it on every sandwich, even on ham and turkey, where others might prefer mayo.

Mustard is by far the most popular of the condiments served with hot dogs. A survey from the National Hot Dog and Sausage Council found that 87 percent of hot-dog eaters prefer mustard as their favorite condiment. The New York Yankees has selected Gulden's—my personal favorite—as their "official" ballpark mustard.

Mustard is made from the crushed seeds of the mustard plant; the leaves of the plant are eaten as mustard greens. Indian mustard seeds, which are brown or black, are spicy. European and American mustard seeds are yellow or white, and milder. A few mustards, such as whole grain mustard and *moutarde a l'ancienne,* are made from whole seeds.

Whether the hull and bran are sifted out during crushing depends on the type of mustard being made. The seed may go through further grinding and crushing.

A liquid—water, wine, vinegar, beer, citrus juices, or a combination of several of these liquids—is added, along with seasonings and other flavorings. The mustard is mixed, in some cases simmered, and then cooled. Some mustard is aged in large containers before it is bottled and shipped to stores.

Mustard seeds are mentioned frequently in early Greek and Roman writings. Romans mixed the seeds with an unfermented grape juice they called *mustum ardens* (burning wine), from which we get the word mustard.

One anonymous ancient author said, "The distressed are quickly cured and the dead resuscitated, thanks to mustard!" Archaeologists have discovered mustard seeds packed in elaborate jars in tombs, an indication that they were used as a ritual offerings to the gods in ancient times.

The ancient Egyptians ate the seeds whole. They took a bite of meat, dropped a few seeds into their mouth, and chewed meat and mustard seed together. Some scholars believe the popularity of mustard seed was due to its ability to mask the taste of spoiled meat. Yuck!

The Romans took mustard seed to Gaul, and by the ninth century, French monasteries had a brisk trade in selling mustard preparations. By the thirteenth century, street vendors in Paris sold mustard from carts at dinner time, much like hot dog vendors sell frankfurters from carts in New York City today.

When a food becomes popular, its production is inevitably regulated by the government. In the sixteenth century, the French government instituted regulations controlling the cleanliness of equipment used in the mustard making.

As new spices were imported to France from the Americas and the Far East, the popularity of mustard declined. But in 1856, Jean Naigeon started making mustard in the city of Dijon with verjuice instead of vinegar, producing a smoother mustard with a less acidic taste. Demand for the new mustard skyrocketed, and Dijon became famous as the mustard capital of the world.

The English also got into the act. One successful British mustard company, Keen & Sons, was founded in 1747. Colman's, still in business today, was also founded in England, in 1804, by Jeremiah Colman, a miller of flour.

Colman separately ground two types of mustard seed— white and brown—and sifted them through silk cloth to separate the husks and the bran from the mustard flour. He originally used black mustard seed, but today Colman's uses brown. After grinding and sifting, the two mustards are mixed together and packaged in the famous yellow tins.

You can make your own mustard at home. Grind a half cup of mustard seed in a coffee grinder or blender until fine. In a double boiler, combine the ground mustard with a quarter cup of lemon juice, half a cup of water, and a pinch of salt and turmeric. Stir until smooth. Heat over simmering water, stirring frequently. Do not allow the mixture to come to a boil. Cool, then thin as needed with extra water.

Like many foods with ancient roots, mustard has been used as a home remedy. Leaf mustard contains calcium, phosphorous, magnesium, and vitamin B. Mustard itself contains no cholesterol, only trace amounts of vegetable fat, and is composed of one-fourth to one third protein. A gram of mustard flour contains only 4.3 calories.

Mustard stimulates appetite, aids digestion, and can help clear sinus passages. Mustard plaster has been used to treat wounds, since it increases blood flow to the inflamed areas of the body. Mustard flour sprinkled in socks is said to prevent frostbite of the toes. In 1982, John King applied for a U.S. patent to use mustard as an acne treatment. Five years earlier, William Vinson had applied for a U.S. patent to use mustard as a baldness cure.

Did Jesus eat mustard? There's no evidence that He did, but we do know His diet was rich in spices. If you want to spice up your diet, try mustard. I have a feeling He would approve.

NATURAL FOODS

~

I'VE BEEN READING A FASCINATING BOOK BY MY FELLOW Thomas Nelson author Dr. Don Colbert. Titled *What Would Jesus Eat?* it advocates a Bible-based eating plan based on the foods that Jesus Christ ate during His life.

How do we know what foods Jesus consumed? In addition to bringing us the Word of God, the Bible is the most widely read history book ever written. And by studying biblical history, we can know with a great degree of certainty what Jesus ate.

For instance, it is fairly certain that Jesus ate bread almost daily. Fish was an important part of His diet. So were fruits and vegetables.

He ate red meat but not the blood or fat. He avoided pork. Olive oil was a staple on Jesus' table, as were goat's milk and honey. Nuts and figs were a frequent snack, as were melons and grains.

Ken Gass, a salesman for Thomas Nelson, told me that after following the Bible-based eating plan spelled out in *What Would Jesus Eat?* the top number in his blood pressure dropped from 210 to 174 in three months. Jan Dargatz, a freelance writer, told me, "Since incorporating these Bible-based foods into my daily diet, I have felt physically renewed—more alive and vital."

As a Christian, you want to do as Jesus did, emulating all aspects of His life, including diet. But how?

Ken told me a simple formula for eating as Jesus ate. Before you put food in your mouth, ask yourself where it came from. Is it "God made" or "man-made"?

Take snacks as an example. Candy is man-made, concocted of chemicals. Jesus never ate it. Honey is "God made," natural—a snack Jesus would eat and surely did eat. The same with raisins.

I don't stick with an all-natural diet all the time. I enjoy certain guilty pleasures, already mentioned elsewhere: specifically, junk food and hot dogs.

But God has given us the healthy foods that can help us lose weight, gain energy, avoid illness, and improve our health. So next time you want to eat healthy, ask yourself "man-made or God made?" And choose the latter for a longer, healthier life.

NATURE

~

NATURE IS THE MASTER DECORATOR, BUT THEN SHE has the finest accessories at her command. Curtains and draperies of silvery mists and rain and multihued clouds; the swags and fringe and vivid accents of leaves. And the rugs she unrolls—floral patterns, the lush green of lawns and pastures, the shimmering gold of the fields, or the deep white fur of glittering snow.

There are no discords in nature. An art teacher once called our attention to the fact that in nature colors cannot clash, as they can on canvas or fabrics. For outdoor light has a quality that blends their native loveliness, whatever the hues. Architects finally discovered that the most beautiful, livable houses are those which allow nature to do much of the decorating through windows which frame the landscape and draw the outdoors in.

—MARJORIE HOLMES, *SPEAK TO THE EARTH,*
HALLMARK CROWN EDITIONS

I like nature, but I am an indoor person. My happiest time is spent in my easy chair reading, or at my computer writing. I live in the world of words, ideas, information, and thoughts.

Perhaps the nature-loving gene in my family skipped a

generation and chose my generation to do it, since my late father was a nature lover, and my older son Alex has followed in his footsteps.

A friend of my father recently commented to me, "Wherever there was water, your father would stop." A lake or stream hypnotized him. If he had a fishhook, a bit of string, and a piece of bread in the car, he would drop it in the water and invariably catch a fish.

Alex is fascinated with water and with animals of all kind—frogs, fish, foxes, bats, deer, coyotes, and chipmunks. We recently moved into a town where deer are seen frequently, and have found a pond where frogs and turtles abound. He is in seventh heaven.

The influence of my father and son are not lost on me. As I grow older, nature's tranquility and beauty hold more allure for me. We recently bought a new house, and one of the things that closed the deal for me was the densely wooded backyard—a nice contrast from the square, all-grass, neat-lawn houses so popular in the suburban towns in my area of the country. We delight in seeing groundhogs, chipmunks, even deer.

When I was a teenager, one summer I worked with a fellow who was a college dropout but constantly quoted one stanza from a William Wordsworth poem over and over again because he was proud he had memorized it. It neatly sums up the grandeur of nature better than anything else I've heard:

One impulse from a vernal wood
Can teach you more of man,
Of moral, evil, and of good
Than all the sages can.

OLD AGE

~

BUT THE DUTY OF LIVING IMPLIES THE DUTY OF remaining young as long as possible. It is by no means certain that all men are convinced of this, so many does one see who settle before their time into a most dangerous state of self-neglect. After all, youthfulness cannot be expected to remain in us without some kind of care. Self-control is necessary at any age, and a young man of twenty who abandons himself to flabbiness is already a wretched spectacle.

Everybody agrees that it is necessary to make one's body obey rules of hygiene; but not everybody asks whether there may not also be rules of mental hygiene. A man who devotes three quarters of an hour every morning to physical jerks, which he usually does badly and which makes him low in spirit, never thinks of washing pointless worries out of this mind, together with squalid little calculations and the dregs of low envy and greed that clog him and harm the sound functioning of his alimentary tract, heart, and nervous system.

But cleaning out one's batteries is not enough; they also have to be recharged. Just as one's cares and worries foul up one's organs, so, necessarily, there are states that favor their rejuvenation. A single word defines them all:

happiness. So long as the quest for it is not regarded as the most imperative duty, its practice taught in the schools, and its name carved upon even the smallest pediments, the future of the human race will still be in jeopardy.

—MAURICE GOUDEKET, *THE DELIGHTS OF GROWING OLD*, THE AKADINE PRESS

For the right to take possession of 90-year-old Jeanne Calment's handsome Aries apartment upon her death, French lawyer Andre-Francois Raffray arranged to pay her a $500-a-month annuity. Actuarial tables would suggest that he had made a shrewd investment, but no. The deal was made known when Jeanne Calment celebrated her 120th birthday, and she became known to be the oldest person on earth. Mrs. Calment reported that she sent Raffray a card every year on her birthday on which she wrote, "Sorry, I'm still alive."

Mr. Raffray died at the age of 77 in December 1995, having paid Mrs. Calment a total of $184,000, almost three times the apartment's value. He's still not off the hook. Under the agreement, his estate has to continue paying Mrs. Calment as long as she lives. "In life, one sometimes makes bad deals," Calment observed philosophically of her lawyer's plight.

—PAUL KIRCHNER, *OOPS!*
GENERAL PUBLISHING GROUP

I heard a story about a man who was about to be executed by a ruthless dictator. Feeling generous, the dictator asked him to choose the way in which he wished to die. "Old age," the man said immediately. The dictator was so amused, he let him go free.

My wife's grandmother, Hazel, is ninety-six. No one in my family has lived to be one-hundred. She may be the first.

I'm not old, but we're all growing older. When I was a teenager and my father was in his forties, I viewed him as old, or at least as "mature." Now I'm forty-four, and I'm not old, but I am aging.

As with most blessings in life, age is a mixed bag. On the con side, I have gained weight and lost hair. I've had some major illness (cancer, stroke), and my muscle tone has gone to flab.

On the plus side, I'm happier and more content than ever. A friend who is a psychotherapist told me, "Once you pass forty, you mentally start to get out of the rat race and off the fast track." I think it's because by forty, you have twenty years of working and achievement behind you, so you've accomplished some of your goals, and feel less pressured to achieve the rest.

Mostly, though, I just like being older. I've said good-bye to teen angst, the intensity of my twenties, and the struggles of my thirties to start both a family and a business. I don't know what's coming next. But I'm looking forward to it with a smile on my face.

PARENTHOOD

~

PARENTHOOD CAN BE BOTH A BLESSING AND A PLEAS-ure—depending on what day of the week it is. But it's always a challenge, and the toughest job we have.

"Clean up your room!" "Stop hitting your sister!" "Go do your homework!" What parent hasn't uttered these phrases over and over, struggling to manage his or her child's behavior?

The problem is that yelling and threatening—a common parental response—are usually ineffective: They cause the situation to escalate, and everyone ends up unhappy. Most of these battles, incidentally, take place either early in the morning (when everyone is rushing off to school or work) or during the "witching hours" of 6 to 8 P.M. (when parents want to get the kids into bed so they can have some time for each other).

As parents, our challenge is to get our children to comply with our requests in a way that does not lead to conflict. The solution: *behavioral management*.

The idea is that children view their behavior as a series of choices they make, and they see that there are positive or negative consequences for these behaviors. You, the parent, can use these consequences to shape your children's behavior and influence their choices.

The first step is to determine what behaviors are acceptable within your family. This is best done at a family meeting, with parents and children sitting around the kitchen table, free from distractions.

Based on the meeting, write out a list of family rules. Give each family member a copy of the rules, and post one on the refrigerator. This list should have between three and six items, and each should be phrased positively. For instance, instead of "no cursing," the rule should read, "Speak nicely to others."

The next task is to work individually with each child on problem areas (target behaviors) of his own. For some children this can be accomplished verbally, but most do well with a behavior chart that is a visual reminder to them of parental expectations and their own behavior.

A behavior chart can be set up one of two ways: rewards for positive behavior only, or rewards and punishment for positive and negative actions. For instance, in the first type of chart, if your child has a problem with cleaning up her room, you would reward her with a star or sticker every day she did it. You would also tell her that when she saved up ten stars or stickers, she would get a reward (go out for ice cream, have a friend sleep over, go to the zoo).

Be wary of promising big rewards, however, because it is amazing how some children are able to motivate themselves when something expensive is promised! The best rewards often have little to do with money, but more with spending time with a parent (such as playing ball, going on a picnic, or fishing).

The second method is to write *yes* or *no* daily beside the target behavior. If the child receives a certain number of yeses that week, he gets a reward. But if he receives too many noes, he loses a privilege (has to go to bed fifteen minutes earlier, doesn't get to watch TV after dinner, doesn't get to play video games after school).

These charts can be quite effective. After several weeks or months, the child should begin to internalize the target behaviors—and not need the structure of the chart anymore to comply. Positive reinforcement, in terms of praise, is important and will lead to a healthy sense of self-worth.

With younger children (ages four to six), don't try to work on more than three target behaviors at a time. Otherwise it becomes too confusing and overwhelming.

For older children, you can target five or six behaviors. When there is more than one child in the family, have charts for all, so one child doesn't feel singled out.

Be creative. There are lots of stars, decals, and cute stickers sold at card and office-supply stores. If you involve your kids in selecting these, they will likely feel happier about this project from the start.

Make the charts from construction paper and place them conspicuously in each child's room. Have a certain time every day to fill them out. Include at least one target behavior on the chart that you know is fairly easy for your child to accomplish. This will help him feel positive about the chart and promote his self-esteem.

Be prepared to follow through with what you say you will do. This is crucial. Avoid making extreme threats ("I'm going to throw your Nintendo 64 in the garbage"). If you write *no* or withhold a star on a certain day, don't let your child talk you out of it. Instead, remind her that you know she's trying—and that tomorrow she'll work hard again. It may be difficult at the beginning, especially if your child is noncompliant. But be patient. The star-chart method almost always brings positive results.

Frame impending behavior as a choice the child is making. If you see a situation escalating, say, "You are up past your bedtime. If you don't get into bed, you are choosing to receive a consequence."

Some parents are able to defuse potential behavior problems simply by saying "star chart" as a reminder. Other families pick a silly, unrelated word (my favorite to use when tempers are flaring is "toothbrush"—a reminder to cool down). Watch out—your children will begin using these words on you as well!

Putting behavioral management into practice takes hard work and willpower. It's tempting, when the kids are whining at full volume, to throw up your hands and say, "All right! Do what you want!" I probably do that way too much.

But when you stick with behavioral management and create clear rules and structures, the rewards of parenting are amplified tenfold or more. You can yell less and have fun more. That's parenting as it was meant to be.

PASSION

~

BASED ON MY EXPERIENCE AND THAT OF OTHERS I
have studied, advised, and consulted, I have learned that
those able to overcome the deterrents to fulfillment derive
their energy and initiative from a single source: passion.
That's right, passion. Not the romantic variety, although
many argue it certainly cannot hurt, but the kind that fills
you with energy and excitement, that gets you up in the
morning and keeps you awake at night.

When you experience it, you lose track of time and
become absorbed in the task at hand. This passion creates
personal intensity, uplifts you, and inspires you. It height-
ens your performance and enables you to achieve things
you may never have dreamed possible.

Most important, it holds the key to your happiness, to
realizing your profit. As Benjamin Disraeli said over a century
ago, people achieve greatness (and, I contend, happiness)
only when they act from their heart and passion. Those who
learn to recognize the promptings of their hearts and then
find the courage to follow them are the ones who win races,
rule nations, and create masterpieces. They also, regardless of
their circumstances, live with a sense of contentment and a
knowledge that they are who they want to be.

—RICHARD CHANG, THE PASSION PLAN, JOSSEY BASS

I recently spoke to a group of several hundred college seniors majoring in engineering. I asked them, "How many of you want to be successful?" Of course, all of them raised their hands.

Then I asked, "How many of you can define success?" Only a few hands were raised.

"Then," I asked, "if you don't know what success is, how can you achieve it?" And I had hooked them for the rest of my talk.

Whatever your definition of success, it has to involve your passions for it to make sense. Who wants to live life doing things they are indifferent or hostile to?

I told the students my definition of success: "To be able to do what I want, when I want to do it, and get paid well for it . . . sometimes very, very well."

What's your definition of success—in business and personal life? What are you passionate about? What turns you on? Find your passion and focus your life around it, and it will be a life well enjoyed and well spent.

A motivational speaker I recently heard said, "There is a powerful driving force within you that, once unleashed, can make any vision, dream, or reality a desire." That force is passion. Pursue your passions in life, and success will follow.

PAUL HOGAN

(Or what you can learn from the man who says, "No worries, mate!")

~

PAUL HOGAN, THE AUSTRALIAN ACTOR WHO PLAYS movie character Crocodile Dundee, inadvertently gives us the best advice ever for attaining peace of mind: "No worries, mate!"

Those who worry don't have peace of mind. Those who have true peace of mind are able to put worries out of their heads. As Henry Wadsworth Longfellow once said, "It's not what happens to you in life; it's how you handle it."

Pop singer Jewel has a great line in one of her songs: "Worry is wasteful." Worrying saps your energy but rarely solves problems. So why even bother?

"All well and good," you say, "but I'm a worrier. How can I make myself stop worrying?" Reverend Louis Conselatore, writing in *Inner Realm* magazine, offers these sensible observations to help you purge worry from your life:

Worrying is futile. Studies have found that 40 percent of our worries relate to things that never occur, 30 percent to things we cannot change, 12 percent to health (while we are still healthy), and 10 percent to petty concerns. Only 8 percent of worries are about real problems. Thus, 92 percent of our worries are wasted.

Worrying is like looking at life through a dense fog. The total moisture in a dense fog one-hundred feet high covering seven city blocks can fit into a glass of water. If we see our problems in their true light, they can be relegated to their true size and place. "And if all our worries were reduced to their true size, you could probably stick them into a water glass too," Conselatore writes.

Worrying is bad for your health. A recent Mayo Clinic study revealed that 80 to 85 percent of their patients were ill directly or indirectly because of mental stress.

Among Conselatore's strategies for avoiding worry:

- Live in the present.
- Try meditation (being alone, quiet, and still for part of each day).
- Help other people.

PEOPLE

PEOPLE CAN BE A BLESSING OR A CURSE—IF YOU LET them. But the fact is, there is good in every person, even the most uncivil and difficult. You have within you the ability to bring out the best in these people and enjoy fruitful relationships with them, if you know how.

Whether or not you are a "people person," you rely on other people every day of your life. You can't buy groceries, read your E-mail, watch TV, listen to radio, read the newspaper, or water your garden without the continuous, active effort of hundreds of different people.

Yet many of us have difficulty coping with other people. Writer Fran Lebowitz says, "I do not work well with others, nor do I wish to learn how to do so." But for most of us getting along with others is a critical skill.

Here are seven habits of people whom others view as having great interpersonal skills. Emulate them today, and your life will be easier tomorrow:

1. *They present their best selves to the public.* Your moods change, but your customer—external or internal—doesn't care. Make a conscious effort to be your most positive, enthusiastic, helpful self, especially when that's not how you feel. If you need to vent, do it in private.

2. *They answer phone calls promptly.* Few things annoy

people more than not having their phone calls returned. Get back to people within two hours. If you can't, have your voice mail guide them to others who can help in your place. If you're really uncomfortable with someone and don't want to talk with that person on the phone, answer his or her query through a fax or E-mail. Or, call when you know the person won't be there and leave the information on voice mail.

3. *They call people by their names and ask questions about their lives.* Take the time to learn and use everyone's name, especially secretaries. Most people don't. You don't have to overdo it, but if you see a child's picture on someone's desk, that person would probably appreciate your asking, "How old is your daughter?" Establishing some common bond makes the other person more receptive to working with you.

4. *They meet people halfway.* Sometimes we're right and the other person is wrong, but I've observed that many people seem to enjoy going out of their way to rub it in the other person's face. Implement the correct solution without making the other person feel stupid or ignorant, for example, "That's a good idea, but have you considered . . . ?"

5. *They listen carefully before speaking.* A sure sign you are not listening to the other person is that you can't wait to say what you want to say, and as soon as the other person pauses, you jump in and start talking. Even if you think you know what's right, listen to the other person. His or her knowledge and grasp of the situation may surprise you. If

not, listening shows you considered the person's opinion and didn't just steamroll over him or her.

6. *They keep eye contact.* When you're talking with someone, look him or her in the eye at various points in the conversation. If you're explaining something to your kids while watching TV, take your eyes away from the screen now and then to look and talk directly at them.

7. *They are not afraid to admit when they are wrong.* Andrew Lanyi, a successful stockbroker, said, "The more you are willing to admit that you are not a guru, the more credibility you gain." No one knows everything, and everybody knows people make mistakes. If you refuse to admit mistakes or pretend to know everything, people won't trust you when you *are* right and *do* know the answer.

May I share a secret? Whether you want to or not, you will have to deal with people every day of your life, from now until the day you die. You cannot change other people; but you can control how you treat them and react to them. A positive attitude in dealing with others can make the coming years or decades a lot more pleasant and productive. It's your choice.

PHYSICAL APPEARANCE

*(If you like the way you look, be grateful you don't
have this problem that I suffer from!)*

~

I'VE HAD LONG HAIR FOR YEARS,
coming out of my nose and ears.

—SEAN MOREY, COMEDIAN

The other day we were driving with the kids in our minivan when my wife shrieked in horrified disgust, "You've got a giant *hair* coming out of your nose!"

I can't help it. As a man ages, hair becomes a problem. I'm simply at the stage where the hair in my nose and ears is growing much faster than on the rest of my body.

You and I each start out with between 100,000 to 200,000 hair follicles on our scalps. Of course, you have more hairs on other places of your body—about three to five million total. Hair grows on almost every part of the body except your palms and soles.

Hair, nails, and skin are similar in structure; hair is, in fact, a modified form of skin built out of a protein called *keratin*. The hair itself is a fibrous shaft. Melanin, contained in small spaces between the fibers, is the pigment that gives your hair its color. As we age, the melanin is replaced by small air bubbles, which cause our hair to turn gray and then white.

Stephen Strauss, author of *The Sizesaurus,* reports that the diameter of the average hair is less than four one-thousandths of an inch across. Each individual hair on your body grows about half an inch a month—over six times faster than your fingernails. The hairs in my nostrils seem to be considerably outpacing this average.

In many parts of the world, excess body hair is not a problem and is actually considered attractive. You can see it on TV during the Olympics, when female athletes from certain countries, when they raise their arms in victory, look as if they have Don King in a headlock. I don't live in one of those countries, but even if I did, I don't think there's a place where ear and nose hair would be "in."

The nose is an especially politically incorrect region as far as excess hair is concerned. My barber routinely trims my ear hair after a haircut, but I'm too embarrassed to ask him to take an olfactory detour with his scissors.

Recently, technology seemed to promise a solution for me. I saw a mail-order ad for a "Quick Rotary Nose Hair Clipper" and sent in my $12.95 with high hopes.

The device looked like a phaser from *Star Trek.* The instructions explained that rotating blades would cut the nose hairs, much like an edger clipping the sides of my lawn.

I inserted the clipper into the offending nostril and twisted. The blades did indeed yank at my nose hairs but did not cut them—and then they locked into position, trapping my nose hairs with their roots still attached to the nostril.

My eyes teared, blurring my vision, as I ran around the house in extreme pain, shouting, "My nose hairs are trapped! My nose hairs are trapped!"

After she stopped laughing, my wife, Amy, said the notion of trying to help me dislodge the offending clipper was too gross for her, and she left the room. There was no way to insert scissors without poking a hole in my septum large enough to accommodate a nose ring I had no desire to wear.

So I took the primitive approach: I yanked.

Now, human hair can be stretched with a force of 29,000 pounds per square inch before it breaks. Arterial walls, by comparison, can withstand only 300 pounds per square inch before rupturing.

According to the book *How and Why We Age,* studies of human scalp hair show that, the older we get, the more the density, diameter, and strength of our hair decreases.

Somehow, though, my nose hairs appear to have confounded this principle. There was a ripping sound as they uprooted themselves, still enmeshed in the rotating blade mechanism of the cutter, from the nostril lining. Some day archaeologists from another planet will find my rotary nose hair clipper amid the detritus of our society. "Looks like a primitive torture device," the alien archeologist will note. "Trapped nose hairs—ugh!"

Since I can't control this unsightly nose hair growth, and conventional hair grooming doesn't seem to offer a solution (should I perhaps braid my nose hair, or tie a bow around

it?), I wonder if nose hairs can be harvested for more productive use. Possibilities include high-strength tensile wire
or transplant material for scalps with receding hairlines.
"Hi," you may hear me say someday on a late-night TV commercial. "I'm not only the president of the Nose Hair Club
for Men . . . I'm also a *client*."

POCKET CALCULATORS

~

THE ADVENT OF THE PC HAS ECLIPSED A SMALLER, humbler invention that, while not as revolutionary, has made life much more bearable for scientists, accountants, engineers, and students worldwide: the pocket calculator.

As a high-school student in the 1970s, I got in on the pocket calculator revolution just in time. We were using slide rules when the first pocket calculators became popular. We gratefully abandoned those clunky slide rules and saved hours doing routine calculations for our math and physics homework.

But the idea of a calculating machine has been around for centuries. Even thousands of years ago, the Chinese invented the abacus, a primitive "calculator" capable of doing addition and subtraction with wooden beads on rods.

Blaise Pascal, born in 1623, was the first man to build a mechanical device capable of performing calculations. By doing so, he laid the foundation for the development of the modern computer. Although today's high-speed computers, with their integrated circuits and sophisticated programs, are as different from Pascal's crude computing machine as night is from day, both are essentially built for the same purpose—performing a lot of calculations at high speed, so some poor worker or student does not have to.

In his calculating machine, known as the "Pascaline," Pascal created a mechanical device to do the work of an abacus.

The Pascaline is a metal device, about the size of a shoebox, consisting of interlocking wheels on various axles. (I say *is* because a few of the devices built are still around today.)

Each wheel has ten notches (just as each rod on the abacus has ten beads), representing the digits 0 through 9. Every time you turn a wheel one notch clockwise, you add a count of one to the digit displayed in a little window above the wheel.

The numbers are painted on small drums. When a wheel is turned, a series of gears transmits the rotation of the wheel to the drum, turning it to the proper digit.

To calculate 21 plus 33, you first turn the right wheel once, and the wheel next to it twice; 21 shows through the windows. Then you turn each wheel three more times to add 33. The total, 54, shows through the windows.

What if you want to perform an addition that requires carrying over, such as 54 + 9? You simply turn the wheel at the far right nine more times, and the total, 63, shows through the windows.

Pascal built into the machine the capability to carry over. When you turn any wheel ten notches, the wheel to its immediate left automatically turns one notch. This is accomplished with a weighted ratchet.

The great blessing of pocket calculators, computers, and

similar devices is that they do routine, dull, repetitive work, freeing the user to *think*. How free do they make you? Calculate 6,473,239.574 divided by 4,562,5586 by hand, and then do it on your calculator. And then give a big tip of the hat to Pascal for saving you the trouble.

POST-IT® NOTES

~

I LOVE POST-IT® NOTES. YOU KNOW, THOSE GREAT little self-stick notepapers. I'm an information junkie, a pack rat, and an obsessive article clipper. Post-it® Notes help me organize my life without drowning me in paper clips.

In today's fast-paced world, time is our most precious resource. And it's nonrenewable: Once it's gone, you can never get it back. Anything that saves you time is a treasure, and for me, yellow Post-it® Notes are pure gold.

Did you know that Post-it® Notes were not a planned product? No one got the idea for them and then stayed up nights to invent it. Their creation was completely accidental.

According to Charlotte Foltz Jones, author of *Mistakes That Worked* (Doubleday), a man named Spencer Silver was working on the 3M research laboratories in 1970 trying to find a strong adhesive. Silver developed a new adhesive, but it was even weaker than what 3M already manufactured.

This weak adhesive stuck to objects, but could easily be lifted off. It was superweak instead of superstrong. No one knew what to do with the stuff, but Silver didn't discard it.

Then one Sunday four years later, another 3M scientist named Arthur Fry was singing in his church's choir. He used markers to keep his place in the hymnal, but they kept falling out of the book.

Remembering Silver's adhesive, Fry used some to coat his markers. Success! With the weak adhesive, the markers stayed in place, yet lifted off without damaging the pages.

3M began distributing Post-it® Notes nationwide in 1980—ten years after Silver developed the superweak adhesive. Today they are one of the most popular office products available.

I'm not smart enough to come up with nifty ideas like Post-it® Notes—on purpose or by accident—or any of the other great products (personal computers, pocket calculators, internal combustion engines) that make my life easier and more comfortable.

I could be jealous of the smart people who invent these things and get rich off them. But I'm not. I'm grateful that God gave them their talents and me mine—even if mine are smaller. I thank them for helping me, and maybe someday something I do will help them. That would be nice.

Problems

～

Sadly we live in a world of ups and downs, and today's laughter can turn quickly into tomorrow's tears. We must learn, and never forget, that wise bit of wisdom passed down to us by some unknown voice of the past who said that a smooth sea never made a skillful mariner; neither do uninterrupted prosperity and success qualify us for usefulness and happiness. The storms of adversity, like those of the ocean, rouse the faculties and excite the invention, prudence, skill, and fortitude of the voyager. The martyrs of ancient times, in bracing their minds to outward calamities, acquired a loftiness of purpose and a moral heroism worth a lifetime of softness and security.

—Og Mandino, *Secrets for Success and Happiness*,
Fawcett Columbine

Some of the things to be grateful for are utter clichés, but also utterly true.

One is the *principle of opposites*, which says, "You cannot appreciate something unless you have also experienced its opposite."

We see this in almost every aspect of life, and examples abound.

For instance, you cannot really appreciate being warm unless you have been cold.

And have you ever noticed how people born to wealth do not appreciate money nearly as much as those who began life without it?

Or how spacious your first big home or apartment feels if you have lived most of your life in a small one?

That's why, rather than avoid problems, we should embrace them.

By solving a problem on our own, we appreciate the solution—and its result—much more than if the problem never existed.

And we also feel a sense of pride and self-accomplishment we would never have if we came upon the positive state of being by mere chance or luck.

I don't go looking for problems, but I don't run away from them either.

How about you?

Seasons

~

IN THE LAST CHAPTER ON "PROBLEMS," WE TALKED about the *principle of opposites*, which says, "You cannot appreciate something unless you have also experienced its opposite."

For this reason I've always appreciated the seasons, and have always chosen to live in a place where the four seasons are distinct and sharply delineated from one another.

Each season has its own pleasures to savor. I don't like the heat, but in summer we get the long days, and what pleasure it is to come home from work and still have daylight in which to play with my children.

In autumn I get my ideal weather—cold but not frigid. As the temperature turns brisk, I become invigorated, filled with new energy. My mood brightens considerably, my mind becomes sharper, and my productivity soars.

Winter is a continuation of the cold weather I love; the snow is beautiful to look at, and the holiday season is filled with joy and good feelings.

In springtime the foliage blossoms, birds begin to sing, the weather is still comfortable, and the days get longer.

Whoever said "variety is the spice of life" hit the nail right on the head.

SELTZER

~

FOR THOSE OF YOU WHO HAVE NOT DISCOVERED ITS pleasures, seltzer—simple carbonated water—is, in my humble opinion, the most refreshing drink on the planet.

My father used to order seltzer every day when he ate lunch at the luncheonette across the street from his insurance office in Paterson, New Jersey. He ordered it by its old-fashioned name—"a two-cents plain."

The name derives, of course, from "two cents"—which was what a glass of seltzer used to cost umpteen years ago—and "plain," referring to the fact that seltzer is unflavored.

Nowadays, nobody calls it two-cents plain. The masses ask for seltzer; the yuppies for club soda or sparkling water.

When we were children, seltzer was delivered to our door in thick, colored glass bottles with squeeze handles. When you pulled the handle, a stream of pressurized seltzer would shoot out. My mother bought flavored syrups—lime, cherry, and lemon—and mixed them with seltzer to make home-made sodas.

Another delight awaiting seltzer lovers is the egg cream, a drink that contains neither eggs nor cream. You put some chocolate syrup in a glass, add a little milk, fill the rest of the glass with seltzer, and stir. It's the smoothest, creamiest chocolate soda you've ever tasted.

Seltzer was invented accidentally in the eighteenth century by the English minister (and amateur) chemist Joseph Priestley. One of his first jobs was pastoring a Unitarian Church in Leeds. As it happens, the parsonage was located next door to a brewery.

Priestley knew that the brewing process generated large volumes of carbon dioxide. He arranged with the brewery to use their waste gases for his experiments.

Priestley put trays of water in the brewing vats. The water absorbed some of the carbon dioxide, making it bubbly. But it had a bad taste—probably from the yeast.

So Priestley made his own carbon dioxide in his laboratory by mixing chalk with sulfuric acid. A glass tube ran from the flask of chalk and acid into a beaker of water. As the carbon dioxide was produced, it ran through the tube and bubbled into the water.

This bubbly water was clean tasting and pleasant to drink. In fact, it was slightly tart and quite refreshing. Does it sound familiar to you? Priestley had invented carbonated water, also known as seltzer or club soda. The Royal Society awarded the Copley medal to Priestley in 1772 for this invention, which also got him elected to the French Academy of Sciences in 1773.

So the next time you are thirsty and want something healthy, refreshing, and natural, raise a glass to Priestley. And make it a two-cents plain.

SLEEP

~

THEN YOU WON'T CARE ABOUT ANYTHING BUT SLEEP
and more sleep. Sleep will be like a woman to you. You'll
always go back to her, because she's fresh and good and
faithful and she always treats you kindly and the same.

—RAY BRADBURY, *THE ILLUSTRATED MAN,* AVON

I firmly believe that early to bed, and early to rise, makes
a man miss pretty much everything good on TV.

—DAVE BARRY

In the middle of the night, when you are sound asleep in
your bed, I am wide awake, envying your slumber: I have
insomnia.

And I'm not alone. According to a National Sleep
Foundation survey, 56 percent of adult Americans report
experiencing symptoms of insomnia a few nights a week or
more—yet only half of these people are being treated by a
health-care provider for their condition. The economic
impact of insomnia in the U.S. is close to $14 billion a year
in lost productivity.

It's not every night, but many nights, and it makes me
mindful of what a blessing a good night's sleep is.

Some people say sleep is a waste of time, and urge us to

get by with less. We sleep one-third of our lives. If you live to be ninety, you will have slept for thirty years.

Others praise sleep, and I'm in their camp. I agree with writer Fran Lebowitz, who in *The Fran Lebowitz Reader* opines: "I love sleep because it is both pleasant and safe to use. Pleasant because one is in the best possible company and safe because sleep is the consummate protection against the unseemliness that is the invariable consequence of being awake."

More and more studies show that getting enough sleep is critical to maintaining good mental and physical health. Sleep's restorative powers are undeniable and easily demonstrated by everyday experience; after a good night's sleep, you feel refreshed and energized.

According to an article in *Adweek* magazine (April 2, 2001), polling conducted for the National Sleep Foundation found epidemic levels of sleep deprivation. While experts recommend that adults get eight hours of sleep per night, Americans average six hours and fifty-four minutes during the workweek. (They get about forty minutes more on weekends.)

In part, the problem stems from people's willingness to jettison sleep in favor of other activities. For instance, 43 percent "often stay up later than they should because they are watching TV or are on the Internet." In other cases, sleep is compromised by problems like insomnia (61 percent of women and 53 percent of men suffer insomnia "a few nights per week or more") or snoring (45 percent of men and 28 percent of women snore).

Twenty-two percent of women are kept awake by a partner's snoring, versus 7 percent of men. Children are an obvious risk factor for sleep deprivation in their parents, accounting for "sleep disruption" in 21 percent of women and 12 percent of men. Given all these problems, it's little wonder that 43 percent of Americans say they're so sleepy "that it interferes with their daily activities a few days per month or more."

So as you fall asleep tonight, be thankful for your ability to sleep through the night. Across the country, in my bedroom, I'll be lying awake and wishing for the same thing.

SPICY FOODS

~

I LOVE SPICY FOODS. IN MY YOUTH, I WOULD HAVE SAID the hotter, the better. Now I say, "All things in moderation." A mild burn is fine, but I'm out of the super hot cuisine for now.

The Turks used crushed red peppers in love potions. Brahmacharya, the principles for attaining purity of soul and body, forbid India's young Brahmans from eating hot peppers. The peppers were believed to produce too much heat in the body system, making blood watery and the mind restless.

Cayenne is primarily used in medicine as a powerful stimulant to increase blood flow and circulation to all parts of the body. It strengthens the heart, arteries, capillaries, and nerves. Hot peppers are also used to treat depression, debility, lack of energy, and any condition caused by reduced blood flow. In addition, cayenne has been proven to lower cholesterol, triglycerides, and blood pressure, and has been found in certain patients to be an anticarcinogen.

Clinical studies have shown that as many as 80 percent of arthritis sufferers experienced significant pain relief with topical capsaicin (capsaicin is the substance that gives peppers their heat). Pain relief occurs almost immediately after the cream is applied to the afflicted area. Published research indicates that capsaicin reduces joint inflammation and nerve sensitivity.

Cayenne's medicinal uses are documented in the United States, Europe, China, and India. It has been used to stimulate the digestive system, to reduce flatulence, to treat cold hands and feet and sore muscles or joints, and in select Native American cultures as a stimulant and to wean children.

They say variety is the spice of life, and when you're eating, spice adds a broader range of taste to your palate. We go to great pains to avoid being bored, and with a well-stocked spice rack, breakfast, lunch, and dinner never have to bore you again.

SUNSCREEN

~

IN HIS HIT SONG OF 2000, BOZ LUREMAN WARNED Americans, "Don't forget the sunscreen." Airman Ben Green invented sunscreen during World War II to protect soldiers against the blazing South Pacific sun.

(Green went on to become a pharmacist and founded Coppertone. He made the first Coppertone consumer sunscreen, using cocoa butter and jasmine, on his wife's stove—and tested it on his own bald head.)

Not only is "Don't forget the sunscreen" good medical advice, but it's also a timely reminder of how human ingenuity can overcome even the most adverse conditions.

Astronomers tell us Earth is the only habitable planet in the universe, and sometimes even on our own planet we're not too safe. There are many regions where extreme cold can kill us. Storms powerful enough to crush buildings and wipe out entire towns abound. Volcanoes erupt and bury villages under lava and ash.

Now even the sun, the source of all energy and nourishment on Earth, threatens our existence.

Pollutants such as chlorofluorocarbons (CFCs) have depleted the protective ozone layer in the stratosphere. Holes in the ozone layer permit too much of the sun's ultraviolet radiation to reach the planet's surface.

Overexposure to UV rays can lead to skin cancer, cataracts, and weakened immune systems. Our very planet has turned hostile—a cancer risk. (I'm among the victims, having had a melanoma removed from my chest last year.)

But we're getting smart and fighting back. Over 160 countries have signed the Montreal Protocol, a treaty that bans CFC production. Scientists are hopeful that the ozone layer will return to normal levels by about 2050.

Until then, cover up, wear a hat, and don't forget the sunscreen.

TECHNOLOGY

~

TODAY, MANY OF THE MOST DRAMATIC SOCIAL AND commercial changes are driven by technological innovations, and therefore we must learn to accommodate the technology that is such an important aspect of our lives. As much as you might wish some days that your pager would stop ringing, can you imagine a life without the ATM machine or voice mail? In most cases, if a new technology does in fact make our lives easier or more efficient, it is here to stay—at least until the next revolutionary innovation comes along. The only sensible thing to do is to get used to it and then to learn to take advantage of it.

—ROBERT STUBERG, *CREATING INTERNET WEALTH*,
NIGHTINGALE CONANT

Technology is a double-edged sword. It solves problems, but it creates problems too.

I'm not complaining, mind you. I love my PC—and the Internet. But some offshoots of computer technology I'm not so thrilled about. Like video games.

Just the other day, for instance, I shouted, "I'm a prisoner of Zelda," mostly to myself, while sitting in our family room. *The Legend of Zelda* is a video game my kids are addicted to.

How does this affect *me*? You can ask only if you are not

the parent of a video-game-addicted child. Parents like me who have made the mistake of allowing a video game system into their homes know all too well the terrors this addictive activity can release.

To begin with, there's what I call "TV Monopoly." I don't mean the video game *Monopoly,* although there is one. I mean that our sons—Alex, 11, and Stephen, 8—play Nintendo and PlayStation so much we never get our turn at the tube. I need *Everybody Loves Raymond* once a week to realize I'm not alone in the battle to be a good parent and spouse; and my wife, Amy, sucks up *Friends* in the same needy way. But now, since Alex, Stephen, and their video games began monopolizing our TV sets, Amy and I have only each other to entertain ourselves nights—and frankly, it's driving both of us crazy.

Then there's "Nightmare on River Road," which is where West Coast Video is located in our town. Our kids love to rent and return games as if there was no tomorrow, leaving us to keep track of due dates and pay both rental costs and late fees. It's a universal law of nature that the return date for any video game is two days before we actually return it. I checked our account with the store last week, and the total we've paid in late fees this year is only slightly less than the gross national product of Kuala Lumpur.

Another game that's great for building family togetherness is "Teach Me, Mommy and Daddy." The boys often reject our offers of help with homework because they want to finish it as fast as possible, and Amy and I have the annoying habit of wanting them to take the time to understand what they're doing.

But the minute they get stuck on a level of *Zelda* or one of their other favorite games, they suddenly yearn for our counsel. "I'm stuck," they'll tell us. "How do I get past this?" I, like the majority of adults age forty and over, am a video-game moron: The minute I start reading instructions, my eyes glaze over. When I take the controls, my character instantly bursts into flame or falls off a cliff, causing my children to tear the controls out of my grasp in contempt. "Dad stinks at video games," Alex tells Stephen, who nods in agreement as he stares at the monitor.

The first video game, *Pong,* was relatively peaceful. Invented by Nolan Bushnell, it involved bouncing a ball back and forth in a tennis-like match. Bushnell founded Atari, an early personal computing company, as well as Pizza Time Theater, a chain of kids' pizza restaurants featuring video games and stage shows with robotic characters (now known as Chuck E. Cheese's).

Video games today are so violent that the industry actually rates them by how much blood is displayed on the screen. Some games even let you turn off the blood, a feature our kids use to persuade us to rent them ones we deem inappropriate because of the violent content.

Psychologists have long argued whether TV violence causes violence in real life, and the argument has now been extended to video fracases. Well, I can tell you point-blank that video game violence *does* promote aggressive behavior; I have seen both my kids and others get abusive with one another, verbally and physically, in a dispute over a game move.

My *favorite* game is "Who Wants to Make the Video Game Manufacturers Millionaires?" The manufacturers play this one well by upgrading systems, it seems, about every three weeks. Of course games for the old system don't work on the new, so you have to buy new versions of the old games at about $50 a pop. The geniuses who run Sony and Nintendo may not have gone to Harvard Business School, but they apparently learned their upgrade strategy from the world's most famous Harvard dropout, Bill Gates.

Naturally, your kids only want to play the new system, so the old system games—which were *also* about $50 a pop— are now an expensive set of plastic blocks. They aren't very good for building, but are great for leaving around the floor so people can step on and break them.

In the movie *Terminator*, Arnold Schwarzenegger tried to prevent super computers from taking over the world by going back in time and killing the inventor of the super computer chip. I thought about doing that to Nolan Bushnell et al., but that would merely support the kind of video game violence I object to in the first place.

Maybe I can track down Bushnell in the *present,* though. We could share a pizza (Pizza Time, if he still bakes them) and talk about the future. At least he'd be talking to *me,* which is more than my kids do when they're playing Zelda.

TELEPHONES

~

ON THE CARTOON SHOW *DEXTER'S LABORATORY*, Dexter's father, tired of his wife talking constantly on the phone, rips the phone out of the wall and exclaims, "I can't stand another minute of this mindless gab!"

While telemarketing calls during dinner or a teenager's marathon phone calls can try our patience, we all recognize the great convenience of modern telecommunications. Great distances are bridged in a millisecond. Wireless telecommunications let us call for emergency help when stranded on a lone highway in the middle of the night, or respond to office E-mails without leaving home.

By following just a few common-sense rules, we can make our time on the phone more pleasant and productive for both our callers and us:

1. *Promptness counts.* Answer your calls on the first or second ring, if possible. This gives the caller the impression that you are responsive and efficient. Occasionally, you may have to delay answering a call to finish an urgent task or because you were momentarily away from your desk. But no office phone should ring more than four times before being picked up by someone. Otherwise, you may risk losing a valuable call.

2. *When you answer, identify yourself.* A "hello" is not sufficient. Give your name: "Bob Bly speaking."

3. At work, follow rule #2 even when picking up the phone for someone else. Say, "Todd Pitlow's office, Mike Bugalowski speaking," so callers will know someone is taking responsibility for helping them.

4. At home, if the call is for someone else, ask the caller to hold, put the phone down, and get the person for whom the call is intended. Do not scream "Mom" or "Steve" at the top of your lungs. It's annoying.

5. If screening calls with your answering machine, do not pick up the phone and take the call in the middle of the message when you realize it's someone you want to talk with. Reason: The caller feels insulted that you are screening his call to you.

6. Answer and place your own calls. Screening calls via a receptionist or secretary wastes time and annoys callers. If possible, answer your own phone. Callers will appreciate the fact that you're available for them and that they don't have to be put through the third degree to reach you. Similarly, placing your own calls circumvents the ego game of seeing which executive waits for the other.

If you must have your calls screened in order to work efficiently, have your secretary do so politely and briefly. Don't make callers feel as if they're being discriminated against. Instead of saying, "Who's calling?" or worse, "Who is this?" which challenges the caller, ask, "May I tell him who is calling, please?"

If you are available to speak to only certain people, ask your secretary to first say that you're in a meeting (if you are) and then ask, "May I tell her who called?" If the caller is someone you want to talk to, your assistant can then say, "Let me see if I can get her for you."

Offer an explanation as to why someone is unavailable. Better to say, "He's in a meeting right now," "She's on another line," or "He's out of the office," than simply "He's unavailable," or "She can't come to the phone." By giving more information to callers, you come across as being honest and up-front, so they are less likely to feel they are being lied to or discriminated against.

Always offer to help the caller yourself, find someone who can, or take a message and personally see that it gets to the right person. Don't ask the person to call back later; this is inconsiderate of the caller's time and money.

When screening calls, avoid using phrases that seem to challenge callers or imply that they may not be worth talking to. For example, the screening phrase, "Does he know you?" is offensive because it puts callers in the embarrassing position of having to guess whether you remember them, and it implies that any caller not known will not be able to get through to you.

People don't like to get the runaround. So if you need to transfer someone, first explain why and where you are switching the call. It's also wise to give the caller the extension or number in case the call gets disconnected.

Finally, realize that although telephones are a great blessing of modern technology, some people see them as an intrusion on their privacy. When in doubt, ask the person you call, "Am I catching you at a bad time right now?" This allows them to gracefully defer the conversation to a more convenient time without feeling put upon. It will win you lots of friends.

TEMPERATURE

~

LOTS OF PEOPLE MAKE INCREDIBLY BIG DEALS ABOUT incredibly small things. For me, it's temperature.

When it comes to temperature, there are basically two types of people in the world: the hot people and the cold people. I'm firmly in the latter camp, and my preference for all things cold has frequently gotten me chilly receptions in mixed company.

You know the hot people: They love the summer. They don sweaters at the first hint of autumn in the air. In winter, they crank up the heat, sleep in flannel pajamas, and put two comforters on the bed.

To us cold people, all of the above is torture akin to being roasted like a barbecued pig over an open charcoal pit.

For the die-hard cold people, summer is nature's version of Dante's *Inferno*. When the first hint of autumn is in the air, we breathe a sigh of relief. "Put on a jacket!" our parents and spouses yell when we go without one on a 40-degree day. At night, we push away the comforters, and—when the other person in our bedroom is fast asleep—crack open the window.

The first person I was ever at odds with because of my being a cold person was my father.

My room was the finished attic space of a three-bedroom Cape Cod. Being an attic space, it became unbearably hot in the summer. I naturally wanted to run the air conditioner full tilt all night.

My father objected that our electric bill would be astronomical. I countered that I couldn't sleep in an oven. We argued, my mother mediated, and I kept the AC on, albeit at a compromised 72 degrees rather than the frosty 66 degrees that really made me comfortable.

Out of guilt at driving up the electric bill, I tried to reduce the heating bill by turning the radiator in my room completely off in the winter. I liked the chill fine, but when the water in my toilet bowl froze, my parents complained that the low temperatures in my room were too extreme.

The second person my cold nature put me at odds with was Matt Schwinger, my first and only college roommate.

Thrown together on the first day of our freshman year, we got along swimmingly until the night of that first day—when we realized that he liked to sleep with the windows closed, while I liked to sleep with the windows open.

We nearly came to blows over it. Our friendship ended and we barely tolerated each other for two semesters. From then on, I made sure I had my own room.

The third person I was put at odds with was my wife, Amy. She is a hot person, and we could never agree on a temperature for the thermostat. She wanted 72 degrees, while I was partial to 65 degrees. But because she could give me something Matt could not—children, a home, and a family—I gave in and kept the window in our bedroom closed on winter and fall nights.

Menopause—Amy's, not mine—has at last brought some cool comfort to my life: Whenever Amy has a hot flash, she becomes too warm and opens the window or turns down the thermostat to create the cool room temperatures I love.

Given the big issues and tragedies in life—both of us having had cancer, the challenges of raising kids, and September 11, 2001—a variation of a few degrees in the room temperature either way is a relatively small thing. Yes, some like it hot, and I'm not one of them. But when they crank the thermostat up, close the windows, and light the fireplace, I no longer lose my cool.

Time

~

DAY, N. A PERIOD OF TWENTY-FOUR HOURS, MOSTLY misspent. This period is divided into two parts, the day proper and the night, or day improper—the former devoted to sins of business, the latter consecrated to the other sort. These two kinds of social activity overlap.

—AMBROSE BIERCE, *THE DEVIL'S DICTIONARY*
OXFORD UNIVERSITY PRESS

I'm looking at my watch. It's 8:38 on a Friday morning. By my calculations, I have only 204,400 waking hours of life left. And I intend to make the most of the time still available to me. How about you?

Today the demands on your time are tremendous. Everyone has too much to do and not enough time to do it. According to an article in *Men's Health* magazine (March 1997), 42 percent of American workers believe they are overloaded with work.

The same overloaded condition exists at home. Children today have so many commitments—after-school programs, extracurricular activities, part-time jobs, clubs, sports, and lessons—that many actually use daily planners to manage their schedules.

It's worse for parents. Not only do they have to chauffeur

these children to all these appointments, but each activity also has a mountain of paperwork and commitment for the parents attached to it. And that's on top of cooking, cleaning, household maintenance, yard work, and dozens of other responsibilities that far outweigh the hours in the day available to complete them all.

We live in the Age of Now. Customers are more demanding than ever. They want everything yesterday. As *Miami Herald* columnist Leonard Pitts comments, "We move faster than ever, but never quite fast enough."

"When our society travels at electronic speed, we fall under the sway of a new force . . . the power of NOW," says Stephen Bertman, a professor at the University of Windsor, in an interview with *Future Times* (Fall 1998). "It replaces duration with immediacy, permanence with transience, memory with sensation, insight with impulse." He argues that this acceleration of change contributes to "a growing sense of stress, disorientation, and loss." On the other hand, if you master strategies for coping with today's accelerated pace, you can meet the demands placed upon you while still having time for yourself.

According to an article in *American Demographics* (January 1999), consumers have come to view time as their most precious commodity: "To satisfy today's consumer, you need to do business in a real-time world—one in which time and distance collapse, action and response are simultaneous, and customers demand instant gratification."

"We've learned to live by the Rule of 6," notes Gary Springer in an article in the *Business-to-Business Marketer* (February 1998). "What used to take six months now takes six weeks; what used to take six weeks now is wanted in six days; what normally took six days is needed in six hours; and what used to be done in six hours is now expected in six minutes." Technology, says Springer, is responsible for much of this change.

Downsizing has left organizations leaner and meaner. Thousands of workers have been fired, and those who remain must take up the slack and work harder than ever. According to a Harris poll, between 1973 and 1993, the average workweek increased from forty-one to fifty hours.

A radio commercial for Bigelow herbal tea observes, "We seem to live our lives in perpetual motion." In fact, we're so busy, we don't even have time to eat! For instance, the "lunch hour" is disappearing from the American business world. Workers more frequently eat lunch at their desks, and 40 percent take no lunch break at all (as cited in *The Futurist* magazine). The typical lunch break is thirty-six minutes, and many people use that time to take care of personal business rather than eat. Recently I read that cereal sales are declining because cereal and milk can't be eaten in the car while driving; breakfast bars meet that need better.

In her book *The Worst Years of Our Lives*, Barbara Ehrenreich writes:

I don't know when the cult of conspicuous busyness began, but it has swept up almost all the upwardly mobile, professional women I know. Already, it is getting hard to recall the days when, for example "Let's have lunch" meant something other than "I've got more important things to do than talk to you right now." There was even a time when people used to get together without the excuse of needing to eat something—when, in fact, it was considered rude to talk with your mouth full. In the old days, hardly anybody had an appointment book.

It's not only women, of course; for both genders, busyness has become an important insignia of upper-middle-class status. Nobody, these days, admits to having a hobby, although two or more careers—say, neurosurgery and an art dealership—is not uncommon, and I am sure we will soon be hearing more about the tribulations of the four-paycheck couple.

You can't jam a twenty-fifth hour into a twenty-four-hour day. Time is a nonrenewable resource that's consumed at a constant and relentless rate. Once an hour is gone, it's gone forever; you can never get it back.

Samuel Butler called time "the only true purgatory," and Emerson said time is "the surest poison." But I disagree. How you use your time is largely up to you. And the best time to start spending your time more wisely? Right now.

UMBRELLAS

~

SAMUEL FOX INVENTED THE FIRST UMBRELLA IN 1874 near Sheffield, England. It featured a curved steel rib frame that formed a shelter when held over the user's head.

At the cemetery where my mother's parents are buried, rabbis are available to say a prayer for the dead. They all seem to carry umbrellas, even on nice days.

One day my father asked the rabbi saying the prayer, "The sky is clear blue without a cloud in it. Why are you carrying an umbrella?" Without missing a beat, the rabbi replied in a serious tone, "It might rain."

To me, the umbrella is a symbol of the instinct God gave us to prepare for the unexpected, an important survival mechanism, especially in today's uncertain world.

Squirrels instinctively know to store food for the winter, even before the food becomes scarce. In the same way, we have the God-given sense to prepare for the worst, so that when crisis strikes, we are not caught unaware and can reduce our suffering to a minimum. The insurance industry, in which my father worked as an agent for forty years, was founded to service just this need.

So be sure to take a tip from the rabbi, and be prepared for a rainy day.

VITAMINS AND HERBS

~

ALTHOUGH AMERICANS NOW SPEND $30 BILLION annually on nutritional supplements, the idea of consuming natural substances for healing goes back to biblical times: Psalm 104:14 says of the Lord, "He causes the grass to grow . . . and vegetation for the service of man." And 2,500 years ago, Hippocrates counseled, "Let food be thy medicine, and medicine thy food."

Using nature's incredible healing power is nothing new. Did you know that thousands of years ago, the ancient Chinese and Egyptians used herbs like ginger and garlic to keep themselves healthy?

Examples of herbal healing abound. For instance, the 5,000-year-old Ayurvedic texts of ancient India recommend guggul, a gummy resin from the boswellia tree, for a variety of conditions including arthritis, diarrhea, and pulmonary disease.

Or consider the growing popularity of St. John's Wort. From the ancient Greeks through the Middle Ages, St. John's Wort was used as a practical folk remedy for treating kidney problems, healing wounds, and alleviating nervous disorders. In 1998, annual sales of St. John's Wort exceeded $127 million.

In the 1500s, cinchona (Indian fever bark) was used to treat malaria and other fever-inducing diseases. More recently, another plant, bilberry, was given to Royal Air Force pilots to improve their night vision when flying nighttime missions during World War II.

Even the pharmaceutical industry recognizes the healing power of plants, although they don't widely acknowledge it. Did you know, for example, that 25 percent of Western pharmaceuticals contain ingredients from plants found in the rainforest?

Most people don't realize so many drugs are derived from plants, because pharmaceutical companies don't advertise this fact—after all, they make a lot of money selling their prescription medicines. But a few years ago, researchers at Roche Vitamins and Fine Chemicals published a study on the benefits of supplementation. Their findings: If all women of childbearing age were to supplement with zinc and folic acid, and everyone over fifty took vitamin E, the annual savings in the United States in hospital charges alone would be nearly $20 billion.

"Many people, both men and women, are now taking herbal products," writes Ann Landers in her syndicated column (*Record*, November 2, 1998). "They are less expensive than prescription drugs and have fewer side effects, and the results have apparently been very satisfactory."

According to an article in *Prevention* (July 1999), Americans now make at least 629 million visits annually to alternative practitioners, compared to 386 million visits annually to family doctors. According to a study published in the *Journal of the American Medical Association* (November 11, 1998), four out of ten Americans have tried alternative medicine.

So yes, an apple a day just may keep the doctor away. Or maybe a cup of green tea instead?

YOUTH
~

Although I'm guessing it was an elderly person who first said, "Youth is wasted on the young," no logical person who clearly remembers his or her youth would agree.

The human life is like a year of seasons. And just as each season prepares the Earth for the next, each phase of our lives is but a training ground for the portion of our lives to come.

In spring, rain and sun awaken foliage that blooms full to give us a glorious summer. In summer and fall, plants grow to provide the animals with food to see them safely through barren winter.

With people, the wisdom we lack in our youth is offset by boundless energy and enthusiasm, fearlessness, and boldness that allow us to accomplish things we don't understand are impossible. Part of youth is not knowing what can't be done, and then doing it anyway. When we're older, our knowledge and accumulated wisdom make us cautious and hold us back. This saves us a lot of grief but also denies us a lot of risk, thrill, and joy.

We should be glad we have the innocence of youth while we are young. Youth is not wasted; it is a once-in-a-lifetime opportunity. Other opportunities come later, with experience and knowledge and care. But youth isn't wasted on the young; it's their greatest gift. The waste would be to allow too much adult wisdom to interfere with this gift and cause us, in fear, to let it lie dormant and unused.

AFTERWORD

~

THE PARADOX OF OUR TIME IN HISTORY IS THAT WE have taller buildings, but shorter tempers; wider freeways, but narrower viewpoints. We spend more, but have less; we buy more, but enjoy less.

We have bigger houses and smaller families; more conveniences, but less time; we have more degrees, but less sense; more knowledge, but less judgment; more experts, yet more problems; more medicine, but less wellness. We drink too much, smoke too much, spend too recklessly, laugh too little, drive too fast, get too angry, stay up too late, get up too tired, read too little, watch TV too much, and pray too seldom.

We have multiplied our possessions, but reduced our riches. We talk too much, love too seldom, and hate too often. We've learned how to make a living, but not a life; we've added years to life, not life to years.

We've been all the way to the moon and back, but have trouble crossing the street to meet a new neighbor. We conquered outer space, but not inner space. We've done larger things, but not better things.

Remember to spend some time with your loved ones, because they are not going to be around forever.

Remember to say a kind word to someone who looks up to you in awe, because that little person soon will grow up. Remember to give a warm hug to the one next to you, because that is the only treasure you can give with your heart, and it doesn't cost a cent.

Remember to say "I love you" to your loved ones, but most of all mean it. A kiss and an embrace will mend hurt when it comes from deep inside of you. Remember to hold hands and cherish the moment, for someday that person will not be there again.

Give time to love and share the precious thoughts in your mind.

—ANNE GODFREY

Pursue, keep up with, circle round and round your life, as a dog does his master's chaise. Do what you love. Know your own bone, gnaw at it, bury it, unearth it, and gnaw it still.

However mean your life is, meet it and live it; do not shun it and call it hard names. It is not so bad, as you are. It looks poorest when you are richest. The fault-finder will find faults even in paradise. Love your life, poor as it is. Humility, like darkness, reveals the heavenly lights. Superfluous wealth can only buy superfluities. Money is not required to buy any necessary of the soul.

—HENRY DAVID THOREAU

In ordinary life we hardly realize that we receive a great deal more than we give, and that it is only with gratitude that life becomes rich.

—Dietrich Bonhoeffer

Gratitude is not only the greatest of virtues, but the mother of all the rest.

—Cicero

The sun is just rising on the morning of another day, one of the first of a new year. What can I wish that this day, this year, may bring to me? Nothing that shall make the world of others poorer, nothing at the expense of others; but just those things which in their coming do not stop with me, but touch me rather, as they pass and gather strength:

A few friends who understand me, and yet remain my friends.

A work to do which has real value without which the world would feel the poorer.

A return for such work small enough not to tax unduly anyone who pays.

A mind unafraid to travel, even though the trail be not blazed.

An understanding heart.

A sight of the eternal hills and unresting sea, and of something beautiful the hand of man has made.

A sense of humor and the power to laugh.

A few moments of quiet, silent meditation. The sense of the presence of God.

. . . and the patience to wait for the coming of these things, with the wisdom to know them when they come.

—W. R. HUNT

ACKNOWLEDGMENTS

~

THANKS GO TO MY PUBLISHER, MICHAEL HYATT, AND my editor, Brian Hampton, for having faith in me and this project, and for allowing me to create it for the service of others.

ABOUT THE AUTHOR

~

ROBERT W. BLY, 44, HAS HAD HIS SHARE OF BLESSINGS and problems. In addition to having a son diagnosed with ADD (Attention Deficit Disorder), Bob has experienced both a stroke and cancer. Yet he maintains a positive outlook on life, thanks to the "count your blessings" attitude fostered in this book.

"My mother used to tell us, when something bad happened, to count our blessings because it could be worse," says Bly. "For instance, if one of us broke a leg, she'd tell us that there were other children who had two broken legs, or worse, couldn't walk. At the time, I thought she was trivializing our woes, but as an adult I realized that she was putting them in the proper perspective. As Longfellow said, it's not what happens to you; it's how you handle it."

Bob is the author of fifty books, including *Selling Your Services* (Henry Holt & Co.), *Internet Direct Mail: The Complete Guide to Successful E-mail Marketing Campaigns* (NTC Business Books), *The Six-Figure Consultant* (Dearborn), and *Getting Started in Speaking, Training, or Seminar Consulting* (John Wiley).

His articles have appeared in such publications as *Direct Marketing, Business Marketing, Direct, Writer's Digest, New Jersey Monthly, Cosmopolitan, Amtrak Express, Computer Decisions, The Parent Paper*, and *Sharing Ideas*.

Bob has given keynote and breakout presentations at many association meetings, including the International Tile Exposition, Mail Order Nursery Association, American Chemical Society, and International Laboratory Distributors Association. Organizations that have hired Bob to give in-house training to their employees include Walker Richer & Quinn, Thoroughbred Software, IBM, Arco Chemical, Foxboro, Metrum Instrumentation, Cardiac Pacemakers, the U.S. Army, and Osteonics. In addition, Bob has successfully sponsored his own public seminars including "How to Get Out of a Slump" and "How to Become a Published Author," aimed at consumers, and "Writing for ISO 9000," aimed at a business audience.

Bob has taught marketing and writing at New York University. He has appeared on dozens of radio and TV shows, including CNBC and *Hard Copy*.

Bob and his wife, Amy, have two sons. The family attends the United Methodist Church of Hackensack, New Jersey.

Questions and comments on *Count Your Blessings* may be sent to:

Bob Bly

22 E. Quackenbush Avenue

Dumont, NJ 07628

Phone: (201) 385-1220 • Fax: (201) 385-1138

E-mail: Rwbly@bly.com

Web: www.bly.com